HOLIDAY SHORE

Books by
Edith M. Patch

NATURE STUDY

Dame Bug and Her Babies

Hexapod Stories

Bird Stories

First Lessons in Nature Study

Holiday Pond

Holiday Meadow

Holiday Hill

Holiday Shore

Mountain Neighbors

Desert Neighbors

Forest Neighbors

Prairie Neighbors

NATURE AND SCIENCE READERS

Hunting

Outdoor Visits

Surprises

Through Four Seasons

Science at Home

The Work of Scientists

HOLIDAY SHORE

by
Edith M. Patch
and
Carroll Lane Fenton

YESTERDAY'S CLASSICS

ITHACA, NEW YORK

This edition, first published in 2020 by Yesterday's Classics, an imprint of Yesterday's Classics, LLC, is an unabridged republication of the text originally published by The MacMillan Company in 1935. For the complete listing of the books that are published by Yesterday's Classics, please visit www.yesterdaysclassics. com. Yesterday's Classics is the publishing arm of Gateway to the Classics which presents the complete text of hundreds of classic books for children at www.gatewaytotheclassics.com.

ISBN: 978-1-63334-051-0

Yesterday's Classics, LLC
PO Box 339
Ithaca, NY 14851

CONTENTS

Storm waves break into spray on the rocks of Holiday Point.

CHAPTER I

WELCOME TO THE SHORE

HAVE you ever spent a day or a summer at a place called Holiday Shore?

Probably not, for most shore places are named for towns, or people, or bays. Yet there are thousands of holiday shores on the Atlantic and Pacific coasts. There are ways by which you can tell them at once, whatever their names may be on maps.

A really fine holiday shore lies at the end of a cove or bay. It will have cliffs of rocks on which gulls rest. There will be big stones sticking up through sand, or shingle, and round cobbles that rattle when the waves break.

A good shore, too, must have a beach—with the shape of a half-moon of wet yellow sand when the tide is out. There you may wade or dig for clams. Or you may look for shells and seaweeds washed ashore when the waves are high. You may also see the tracks of gulls that come to find food.

In the shallow water, plants and animals live. One plant you are almost sure to see is called eel grass. Look in eel-grass tangles for the pink and brown bodies of jellyfish. You may take the pink ones up in your hands, but catch the brown ones with a pail or net. They have many special cells in their bodies that sting, and the stings hurt for a long time.

In the sand among the eel-grass roots are little lumps that move. Dig under one and you will find a snail that draws its soft body into its shell as you pull it out of the sand. Other snails crawl on the bottom, eating very tiny plants.

Perhaps you will find a larger lump, and will dig out a big, gray king crab with a long spine on his tail. This is Limulus. His race has lived in the sea for more than a hundred million years. You will wish to meet him again, and learn some of his strange habits.

When the tide is as low as it will go, you will hunt among the rocks that lie on Holiday Shore. Watch out for the barnacles! They could do nothing to hurt you if they tried; but if you slip on their rough shells, you may get some cuts.

As you climb about among the rocks, you will find bunches of brownish-green seaweed. Don't forget to lift them, for many things live under these weeds while the tide is out. There are snails, crabs, starfish, and even little fish called blennies. There are also many purple mussels that fasten their shells to the rocks with threads.

What is this—a snail with claws? No, it is a little hermit crab. His body has no shell of its own, so he lives in one left by a snail. He is a timid creature and will do his best to get away when you find him in a crack between rocks.

Jellyfish

Of course you will look for fish that come and go in the water and for birds that come and go in the air. You will no doubt try to find all those mentioned in this book. Perhaps you will think it a good game to count all those whose names you do not find on these pages. One small book cannot tell about all the creatures on and near the shore. The shore itself is the place to study them.

Keep watch of the water beyond the rocks. It is higher than it was an hour ago. That means the tide is coming in. Twice each day of twenty-four hours it goes out and returns, sometimes very, very fast. For your own safety find out how fast the tide comes in when you plan a day at Holiday Shore.

As you walk back over the rocks, you find many green and purple snails. You also see pretty pools where pink and brown plants grow on the rocks, and bright red worms live in shell-like tubes.

While you watch, the water comes up to these pools and spreads over part of the sandy beach. The sea is covering Holiday Shore and you must go away for a time. But the plants and animals that live on the rocks remain and take their food, for their mealtime lasts as long as they are covered with water.

CHAPTER II

THE CHANGING SHORE

THE road to Holiday Shore runs through meadows and past the farm at the foot of Holiday Hill. Then it winds through woods and crosses a stream. This is the stream up which the alewives and some other fish swim to lay their eggs in Holiday Pond.

At last the road comes near the sea. On windy days you can hear the waves as they break on the rocks. When the big waves come in and break like that, you can see how Holiday Shore was made, and why it changes every year.

For the shore really does change. Look at that rocky point: it was once bigger than it is to-day. To be sure it seems firm and unchangeable while the water of the quiet sea ripples on the rocks at its foot. Even on stormy days the point still holds itself strong and steady against huge waves that roll in from the bay. They dash against its hard gray stone and splash into fine, white spray that the wind carries far inshore. How can waves that break into weak misty spray change the shape of Holiday Point?

Holiday Shore

Stand behind this old, twisted tree and see a little of what storm waves can do to the shore. Here comes a big one now; watch it fill every hole and crack. Will it succeed in pushing the rocks apart?

After the wave has broken against the point and the water has run back toward Holiday Bay, you will see pieces of rock come loose and whirl away in the water. Every piece leaves a crack to mark the place from which it fell. When these cracks become deep enough, larger blocks of stone will be loosened to fall from the cliff. You may find blocks on Holiday Point that seem almost ready to fall.

6

When they go down, they will lie among the other rocks in the foaming water. Waves will bump them together, small rocks will be pushed against them, and sand will be scrubbed over their faces. All this rubbing will wear away rough bits from the rocks. It may take only a year or so for the waves to turn sharp-edged rocks into rounded stones like those that lie on the sandy part of Holiday Shore.

Waves pound the cobbles against one another
until they become smooth and round.

Stones worn round by water are called cobbles. Some cobbles are very large. They are blocks that fell from the cliff only a few years ago. Others are small and very smooth. They have been tossed and pounded so

7

long that most of their mass has been carried away. A few were dropped by melting glaciers[1] that once came down from the north and covered the cliffs of Holiday Shore. When the glaciers dropped them, these stones were scratched, but waves have worn their faces smooth.

You can hear the cobbles being ground together. A strong wave rolls up the shore. Listen as the wave breaks and the water runs back to the sea. Clatter-clatter-clatter go the cobbles as they roll about and hit one another. And clackety-clackety-clack go the pebbles that once were cobbles themselves, but have been worn down until they are little. Some day they will be only grains of sand as tiny as those on the beach that covers part of Holiday Shore.

So you see how waves may change the coast. Once it was a straight line of cliffs. Then the waves found a place where they could break off chips of rock, and let big stones fall into the water. They kept this up year after year. In time they dug a little cove. After hundreds and thousands of years, the cove grew big enough to be a bay. You have seen that it is still growing to-day as the waves break on its shore.

What happened to all the rock and sand that was dug out to make Holiday Bay? Part of it was worn so very fine that it drifted far away on the waves. When it did settle to the bottom of the ocean, it was many miles from shore. Much stayed in the bay itself. A great deal still lies on the shore or in the shallow water near by.

[1]See the chapter about "The Old Boulder," in the book *Holiday Hill*.

To study the sands of Holiday Shore, we shall come on a quiet, sunny day. We should choose a time when the tide is low, so that we can walk along the beach and wade far out in the shallow water.

*Water, rippling in the breeze, makes these marks
on the sand of Holiday Shore.*

We may dig holes in the wet sand, finding worms, sand dollars, and white-shelled clams that spend their lives burrowing in it. It is not well to waste the clams. So, unless you wish to cook them for a meal, throw your clams back into the water or give them to people who may use them for food.

As your spade turns up sand from the beach, you

9

find that it lies in layers or beds like many rocks that stand on land. Some layers go this way and that, as the waves or currents dropped the sand. If you pry or dig into the bedrock of Holiday Hill you may find stones that show the same kind of crisscrossed layers. Then you will know that they were formed near shore very, very long ago.

Now let us go to a place where the water hardly covers the sand. It ripples under the summer breeze—and looking at the beach we find ripples like those in the water.

This piece of old sandstone shows ripples
made by waves millions of years ago.

If the sand were to become hard stone, most of those ripples would be preserved. There are many places where you can find sandstones that are millions and millions of years old. And they show the marks of rippling waves like those we now see on the beach even though they may be miles from any ocean. Surely in the ages when the earth was young the sea waves must have rippled over countless shores that are now far inland.

As the coast changes and is worn by waves, the things that live upon it change their homes. When Holiday Shore inclosed a little cove, barnacles and rock mussels lived where we now find sand with seaweeds and clams. Perhaps a hundred years from to-day that cliff will have crumpled and become a pile of cobbles where snails and crabs will crawl.

CHAPTER III

LOW TIDE

WHILE the tide is high, water covers much of Holiday Shore. Bright-colored fish swim among the rocks. Snails crawl about eating plants. Pink and blue starfishes hunt for clams, while seaweeds nod their red and green fronds. Plantlike animals attached to stones spread their legs and tentacles (flexible organs of touch) to catch food.

When the tide is low, all this is changed. Seaweeds hang limp and motionless from Holiday Cliff. Little fish hide in wet cracks and big fish swim away in the bay. Many snails hide under stones, and so do the starfishes and crabs. The shore seems to lie asleep, waiting for the tide to return.

But the animals that burrow in the fine sand are not asleep. Those holes over there were dug by clams and if you stamp your foot near them the clams will squirt water and you will know that they are awake. Those wrinkled lumps of mud were brought up by long green worms that live in burrows under the sand.

If you dig farther out, you will find sand dollars.

They are circular flat creatures with very thick shells covered with silky brown spines. In deeper water they live on the bottom. Codfish and haddock visit Holiday Bay just to get meals of sand dollars.

There are pools on the shore where creatures swim, crawl, and eat, no matter how low the tide may be. These are hollows or basins worn in the rock near the foot of Holiday Cliff. When the tide goes out, water still remains in these hollows. That is why we call them "tide pools."

Let us visit one of these pools while the rest of the shore is free from water.

The rocks around the pool are covered with thick bunches of brownish-green seaweed. In the water float some bright purple sheets. They are the fronds of seaweed called "dulse," which many people like to eat. If you go to grocery stores in seashore towns, you may find baskets of dried dulse for sale. It has a musty, salty taste and it will make you very thirsty if you eat any of it.

On the rocks at the bottom of the pool are hard, rough patches of pink. They are made by a strange seaweed that covers itself with colored lime. Some seaweeds spread out on flat stones. Others, like those in that corner, form lacy fronds of lime.

Those plants that look like huge brown leaves have drifted in from Holiday Bay. The biggest seaweeds in this Eastern bay have fronds that are two or three feet long. But if you visit the coast of Washington, you may find seaweeds called kelp that sometimes are hundreds of feet in length. One of them has a cluster of fronds fastened to a big, hollow ball. This ball is on the end of a stem so long that it reaches to the bottom of the bay. There it anchors the kelp to a stone. Sailors sometimes have thought that these long, twisting stems were brown sea serpents.

Seaweeds, of course, are not really weeds. They have no roots or true leaves. They never have flowers or seeds. Seaweeds belong to a very ancient group of plants called algæ (al-jee). Algæ began to live in the sea millions of years before there were grasses or trees or plants of most other kinds on land. Even now, most algæ live in the sea or in streams and shallow ponds of fresh water.

Those sharp, rough shells fastened to rocks in our tide pool belong to animals called barnacles. Barnacles often live on rocks so high that they are left dry by the low tide. Then they close their shells and wait for the water to cover them before they can have anything to eat.

There in the pool, too, are tubes built by little worms with red gills. They cannot come out and crawl away, like the worms you found burrowing in the beach.

What are those pretty, checkered mats? They are the homes of creatures so plantlike in appearance that they have been given a name meaning "moss animals." Some of their relatives live on the seaweeds that float in Holiday Bay.

Sponges also are animals, even though they look like plants in the pool. Some are green, while others are yellow or pink. Each sponge has a great many tiny mouths, through which it sucks in water and food.

When it has eaten as much as it can, it sends the water out through another larger hole.

In a shady corner of the pool are some large sea anemones (a-nem'-o-nies). Some of them have been scared by a crab. They have shut their mouths and drawn in their tentacles and now look like red and green tomatoes sitting in the water. Other anemones were not frightened by the crab. They sit in the shelter of the floating seaweeds with their mouths open and their fluffy tentacles out, ready to catch food.

Some sea anemones in a corner of the tide pool

Though it is pretty and flowerlike and is named for a flower, the sea anemone is an animal. It is a relative of the corals that build banks and reefs in the sea near Florida. Other relatives are the pale pink jellyfish that swim in the shallows of Holiday Bay.

Some sea anemones cover their bodies with pieces of broken shell. When they close their mouths you can hardly tell them from rubbish that has been caught in a crack.

Some sea anemones cover themselves with pieces of shell.

How do sea anemones eat? Watch this big one when a little fish swims near. His tentacles wave and stretch. Three of them catch the fish and sting it so it cannot swim. Then other tentacles get to work. They pull and push the little fish into the anemone's mouth. He will eat all of it but the fat before he is ready for another meal.

At one end of the tide pool the bottom is covered with sand. There lies a long purple creature with branched tentacles at one end. Five double rows of suckers run the whole length of his body. As he stays there undisturbed his body grows longer and longer, till it looks like a huge purple worm. If you pick him up, however, his body becomes short and stiff. He does not bite or sting.

This queer creature is a sea cucumber. It is a distant cousin of the starfish, even though it looks more like a worm.

The sea cucumber is a relative of the starfish
even though he looks like a worm.

There are other sea cucumbers in Holiday Bay, but most of them live in the mud or sand. They swallow a lot of it every day, to get the bits of food it contains. That means a great deal of work for a little meal—but they are sure of getting something to eat.

The strangest animal in the tide pool is the little white tunicate, or sea squirt. When a baby, he swims freely about in the bay. He has a head, eyes, and a long tail. Down his back runs a piece of gristle like that which in higher animals comes before the backbone is developed. It means that the baby sea squirt is related to fish and frogs.

But this gristle never becomes a backbone. After swimming about for a while, the sea squirt settles down

Sea squirts look like little vases with two spouts.

18

on a stone. He fastens himself by his head, and loses his eyes and tail. Soon he looks like a little vase with two spouts.

Into one spout he sucks water containing food. From the other he sends the water out after he has taken all he can eat. The animal that once seemed to have the promise of a backbone now lives and eats like a sponge!

One sea squirt in the pool near Holiday Shore even buds much as a plant does and forms colonies somewhat like those of the "bread-crumb" sponge.

But why call him sea squirt? Pick up a pebble to which one of these little animals is attached. Squeeze him suddenly. Watch him squirt water two or three feet across the pool. Could you give him a better name than the one he has?

If you go to a tide pool on the Pacific coast, what will you expect to see?

You will find barnacles, seaweeds, and snails. The barnacles will not be quite like those on Holiday Shore. The seaweeds will be bigger. Some of them even may be kelp that waves have washed in from the bay.

You will see many moss animals and creatures that resemble them, though they are really relatives of the corals. You will find purple clams on the shore above the pool, and yellow or red sponges in it. You may think that many of the animals are much like those in the pool on Holiday Shore.

Yet you will find many things that are different. Most of the sea anemones are green; more of the sponges are red. The crabs are purple with green spots. Their shells are longer than those of the crabs in the pool near Holiday Cliff.

Western sea cucumbers are very large, but their tentacles are short. The commonest one often lives in pools. He is long and red, with purple and orange lumps on his skin. If you pick him up, he becomes so slimy and limp that he may slip out of your hands.

Many of the starfish are purple, too. Instead of living in the pools, they like to crawl between cobbles, where they are covered by clumps of damp seaweed. Sometimes you may find five or six, all crowded into one corner.

You will find purple clams on the rocks above the pool.

The most common sea squirt in Western pools is bright red, with a tough, wrinkled skin. Often it is so dirty that you may think its color is brown. A big one will squirt five or six feet if you squeeze him quickly and firmly.

We may spend a long time watching the animals and plants of either a Western or an Eastern tide pool. Even then we shall miss many of them unless we hunt with a microscope. Every sea plant and animal we have met in this chapter begins its life as a very tiny creature that spends its days floating or swimming. Some plants, called diatoms, never do grow big enough to be seen without a microscope.

These young and tiny animals and plants are eaten by their big neighbors. When sea squirts suck and barnacles wave their legs, they are carrying animals too small to be seen into their hungry mouths. Moss animals feed in the same way, and so do worms and clams.

What do the tiny animals eat? Some eat their still tinier neighbors. But those neighbors must also have food. Where do they get their meals?

The affair really starts with plants—both the little ones that float all their lives, and larger ones like scums and seaweeds.

Plants cannot think, neither can they feel as animals do. But they do one thing that no animal can do—they make their own food.

A seaweed or a diatom eats water (which is made of

oxygen and hydrogen) and a gas called carbon dioxide that is contained in the water. You know this gas, which gives soda water its "bitey" taste.

Next, the plant uses sunlight. With the sunlight that comes into a tide pool, green cells in a seaweed turn the water and gas into one of the many kinds of sugar. Then they change that sugar into still other foods, such as starch.

In this work, part of the carbon dioxide is not used. So the seaweed or diatom throws it away in the water. That part is the gas called oxygen. Snails, crabs, sea anemones and other sea animals breathe this gas. Some people believe that no animals could live in the sea until plants had time to throw away a lot of oxygen for them to breathe.

Here, then, Holiday Shore's food chain begins. Plants are nourished by the food they make from gas and water during the day while the sun shines. Sunlight, like dissolved gas, is more plentiful in shallow water near shore than in the deep waters of the ocean. Also, the shore offers protection for animals like barnacles, snails, and crabs.

Now you see why Holiday Shore is such a good place to find plants and certain animals of the sea. It gives them more food, more light, and more shelter than they would find on the bottom of the deep ocean, or even in Holiday Bay. It is because they find the sort of home they need there that animals and plants of so many kinds live on the rocks, in the pools, and even in the sand that make up Holiday Shore.

CHAPTER IV

ASTER AND SPINY

Aster

ASTER, the starfish, was hungry.

Aster was hungry so often that he did not wait long between meals. His favorite food was the mussels with dark purple shells and orange flesh. Thousands of them lived at the foot of Holiday Cliff. They could not hide or run away, for they had fastened themselves so firmly to the rocks that they could not pull themselves loose in time to escape.

As Aster was ready for dinner or luncheon, he walked to a colony of the purple mussels. How do you suppose he walked? Not by moving the five points or arms of his star, as you can move your hand by "walking" with your fingers. When Aster was ready to travel, he used hundreds of little, soft tubes on the under side of his queer body.

Each tube was about three-quarters of an inch long. It ended in a round sucker that could catch hold of rocks or shells. By stretching out some tube-feet and letting go with others, Aster managed to crawl over the stones. When he was going at top speed he walked six inches in a minute. But he did not walk steadily as fast as that, since he often stopped to feel things that were in the way. It was only when he was in a great hurry that he walked as far as twenty feet in an hour.

Of course he had to guide the movements of his many tube-feet. Otherwise he might crawl out into Holiday Bay instead of reaching the rocks where the mussels lived. He could not look to see where he was going although he had five eyes—one small red speck at the tip of each of his five arms. The best these eyes could do, however, was to tell light from darkness, so they were of no help to him in hunting for something to eat.

As Aster crawled, he stretched out a feeler from the tip of each arm, near an eye. These feelers looked much like tube-feet though they had no suckers at the ends. Aster groped here and there with his feeler-feet, somewhat as a blind man feels with his hands or his cane. These strange little organs had more than a sense of touch. They had a sense of taste, much like a sense of smell, as well. So by groping and smelling, Aster found his way to his food without needing eyes to help him.

When Aster came near them, the mussels shut their shells just as tightly as they could. But that did not bother the hungry starfish. He straddled a mussel, humped his body over it, and fastened the suckers of his tube-feet to its shell. Then he began to pull. For a

*This starfish is trying to turn over. He was eating
purple-shelled mussels even when the tide was out.*

while the mussel kept its shell shut; but Aster pulled and
pulled and pulled until finally the purple shell opened.

At last the starfish was ready to eat. But he could
not put the mussel into his mouth, or tear it to pieces
as Hermit, the crab, tears clams. How was he to get his
meal?

Aster had his own way of eating. Squeezing some
muscles inside his body, he pushed his stomach out
through his mouth! Soon the stomach covered the open
purple shell and the bright orange body inside. Then

it began to digest that orange-colored food and in this way Aster got his nourishment. When nothing was left of the mussel but the shell, Aster drew his stomach back into his body again, and went off to rest under some seaweeds.

Aster did not really know much about what was happening near him. With eyes that sensed no more than a difference between light and dark places, he could not really see his neighbors. And though he had all the nerves he needed, he had no brain and could do no thinking. He did not even get very well acquainted with Mrs. Aster, who also came to Holiday Bay and laid many thousands of eggs in its shallow water.

Mother Aster's eggs floated in the water. They hatched into tiny, colorless things shaped somewhat like bunches of little thumbs. They could swim by means of movable hairs, but most of the time they merely drifted about. When currents or waves brought them close to the shore, some of them were pulled into the mouths of barnacles or mussels. This happened so quickly that they knew nothing about it.

After a time the infant starfish that had escaped being eaten stopped drifting and caught hold of seaweeds or eel grass. There they ate, grew, and changed into blunt, five-pointed stars. Soon they were shaped enough like Mother Aster to resemble her, though they were still very, very small. When they dropped among pebbles and rocks, they began to creep on tiny tube-feet and hunt for food.

The young starfish did not need to be very particular

about their diet. They ate baby barnacles and baby clams part of the time. For some of their meals they ate bits of decayed things they found on the bottom of the bay. In this way they helped keep the places near them clean and such food did them no harm whatever.

You may think that all Mother Aster's children would be pink, as she was. Some of them were, but others were orange or brown, and a few were red or blue or purple. Young brother and sister starfish of this kind may have complexions of very unlike colors.

Every little while one or another of Aster's brothers or sisters had an accident of some sort. Quite often a hungry fish would come near enough to nip off an arm. The loss of a mere arm or two, however, is not so serious

*One of Aster's arms was eaten by a crab
but a new one soon began to grow.*

27

a matter to a starfish as you might think it would be. Aster himself was once caught by a big crab and seemed in danger of being torn in two.

How do you suppose Aster escaped? He simply let go of the arm that the crab held. Then he crawled off to hide among rocks. Soon the wound healed and a new arm began to grow. In time this became as large and as strong as the arm that was eaten by the crab.

When the tide goes out, Aster and others of his kind lie under bunches of cool damp seaweed. Since they do not crawl very far, a number of them often crowd together beneath the same shelter. Lift a bunch of seaweed and you may find seven or eight starfish, all squeezed into one corner. Look to see if some of them have small arms growing to replace arms they have lost.

If you live on the Pacific coast, you will not meet starfish just like Aster on the rocks. Instead, when you lift the seaweeds, you will find several much bigger purple starfish. Turn one of these over and you may see that he can eat even while the tide is out, for he will probably be holding a mussel or two within reach of his stomach.

You also can see how he uses his tube-feet to turn himself right-side-up if you lay him on his back. First he twists his five arms. Then he reaches out with his feet and begins to pull. In much less time than you expect, he turns himself over and lies on the rock, ready to eat another meal.

Aster has many relatives in the sea and some of them come to Holiday Shore. Two of these relatives

*When you lift the seaweeds you may find
several big purple starfish.*

are called sun-stars. They have big, round bodies and more arms, or rays, than Aster has.

One sun-star is dark red. Its skin is rather smooth and it has from nine to eleven slender, pointed arms. You sometimes will find it in deep tide pools or will see it lying under water on the rocks below Holiday Point.

Beside the dark red sun-star in the tide pool you may find a very spiny sun-star with as many as fifteen arms. Its body is covered with bunches of little spines, with longer spines on the sides of the arms. Its color is buff or pink, with spots and lines of red or purple. This spiny starfish in Holiday Bay is generally small but on the Pacific coast there is another spiny sun-star with fifteen to twenty arms that often grows to be two feet across. Sometimes a giant starfish of this sort is even twice as large as that—the very biggest starfish in the world.

Spiny

Still another of Aster's relatives lives on the rocks near Holiday Point. He likes to stay where the water is so deep that low tide will not leave him dry, though he may also be found in some of the tide pools at the foot of Holiday Cliff.

This relative is Spiny, the green sea urchin. As he lies on the bottom of a tide pool, Spiny looks like a flattened ball of spines. Watch him closely and you will see that the spines move. You know, then, that they are fastened to something beneath, with muscles that move them to and fro.

Spiny has a hard, nearly round shell in which there are many holes. Through some of these holes he breathes. Inside a big hole, at the center of his under side, is his mouth with its five strong teeth. On his top and sides are many small holes through which Spiny pokes long tube-feet.

You will see all these holes if you find an empty shell lying on the sand of Holiday Shore. You will also

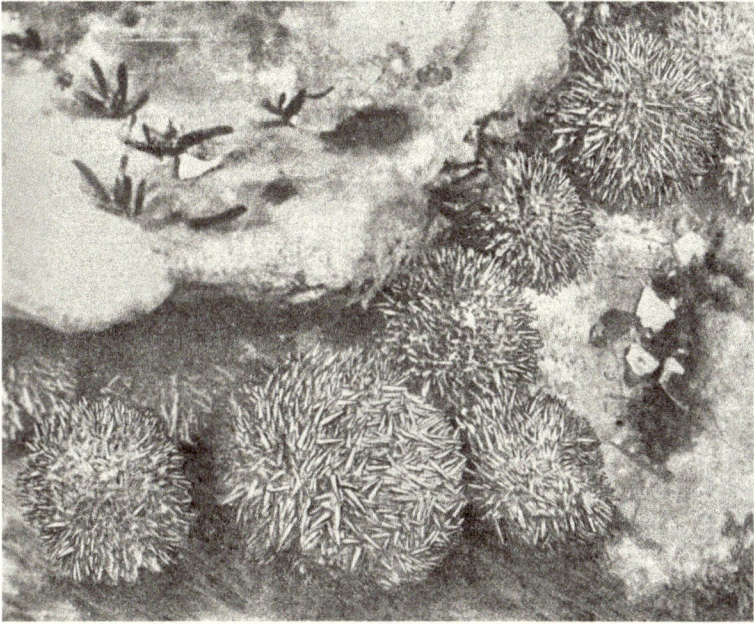

A group of green sea urchins

see many shiny knobs, to which the sharp green spines are fastened.

By means of these spines the sea urchin walks. With strong muscles he moves them about, like a boy walking on stilts. Spiny, however, has many stilts, not two only, and he is in no danger of falling. If the stilts do not work fast enough, he reaches out with a dozen or more tube-feet and pulls himself over the rocks.

Just now, Spiny is eating a meal. He has found a patch of mosslike animals that are relatives of the sea anemone. He cuts them with his five white teeth. Pieces that might float away are caught by many little pincers among his spines. With his tube-feet Spiny takes these bits from the pincers and puts them into his mouth.

31

Some of the other sea urchins are eating the green plants that cover many of the rocks. Crawling as they eat, they leave bare trails across the surfaces where they live.

If a sea urchin gets plenty to eat without moving, he may sit for weeks or even months in one spot. His spines and teeth scrape the rock away while he eats, until he settles into a deep cup-shaped hollow. While he is digging, day after day, the sea urchin grows, so he makes his hole bigger at the bottom. Sometimes you may find old sea urchins that cannot get out through the small openings at the top of the caves they have made while feeding.

Spiny is a little sea urchin not more than two or three inches wide when full grown. His spines are short. There are sea urchins belonging to this same species, or kind, living in many parts of the sea. Children on the shores of Germany watch urchins like Spiny in the tide pools. Eskimo boys and girls see them in Greenland. If you should travel along the Pacific coast, you would find Spinies of the same kind all the way from Washington to Alaska.

You would find urchins of two other kinds along the northern Pacific coast also, one that looks like a little purple brother and another three or four times as large as Spiny with long red or purple spines. But not even this large sea urchin has spines as long as those of a kind living on the coast of Ireland. An urchin that an Irish child might find has spines longer than its body is wide.

Here is something interesting you will wish to

know about Aster and Spiny: They belong to the only important group of animals that has never ventured into fresh water or lived on land.

You can find some worms, snails, crabs, and so on, dwelling in creeks, ponds, and on land, while some of their relatives remain in the ocean. But neither land nor fresh water tempts a starfish or a sea urchin of any kind. They all still remain in the sea where they have lived for millions of years.

English children often dig in the sand for cake urchins. These creatures have hundreds of velvety spines, and crawl along just under the sand. Instead of biting off plants, they shovel sand into their mouths, eating tiny creatures that live in it. You have seen that some sea cucumbers get their food like this—and they are distant cousins of the cake urchin.

Heart urchins live in sand, too. They dig holes about nine inches deep, using their short, flattened spines. They plaster a chimney leading up to the water, using a sort of glue that they make. Their food must come in through that chimney, while the heart urchin lies in wait. A lazy way of living? Of course, but the heart urchin seems satisfied!

CHAPTER V

SHORE SNAILS

The Moon Snail's Meal

MANY empty snail shells are washed up by the waves and lie on Holiday Shore. Some of them have long, sharp points. Others are blunt with ridges on them. There are still others that are nearly round and rather smooth. They are white or blue-gray or brownish and the largest are four inches long.

These large, smooth shells were built by moon snails. Moon snails never crawl on the rocks; but if you look closely on Holiday Beach you may see the tip of a shell sticking up through the sand. As you watch, it moves. The moon snail is able to crawl, even when it is buried in sand.

Would you like to see a moon snail crawl? Then dig one out of the sand with your spade and put him in a shady tide pool. At first he will lie quite still, with the mouth of his shell closed by a brown door. Soon that door will begin to open. If nothing scares him, the moon snail comes out ready to take a walk.

A Moon Snail

Did you ever suppose such a big body could come out of this pretty shell? It rolls out and begins to spread. Soon the shell almost disappears in this great mass of pearly flesh.

But not all of this huge body is flesh. A great deal of it is water that the snail pumped into his body while he was getting out of his shell. When you disturbed him a little while ago by digging him from the sand, he squeezed most of the water out and so could tuck his body away.

Taste guides him to some fish meat lying on the stones. Hermit crabs have been feasting there, tearing off bits with their claws; but they run away when the moon snail comes near. There is nothing to interfere with him, so he spreads his big body over the fish and settles down for a good meal.

The last time the moon snail had something to eat, he was buried in the sand of Holiday Shore. As he crawled through it he met a clam, which quickly closed its hard white shell.

Did that discourage the moon snail? Not at all. He wrapped his body around the clam and stuck out his horny, sharp tongue. As he moved it, his tongue bored a neat hole through the shell of the clam. Then the moon snail reached in with a pair of sharp jaws and began to eat the juicy clam meat. In an hour nothing was left but the shell, with the hole that the moon snail's tongue had bored.

If you look at the empty shells on Holiday Beach, you will find many that show just such holes. Some are the shells of the purple mussels that lived on the rocks near Holiday Point. Others are the shells of "hard-shell" or "soft-shell" clams that burrowed in the sand near the shore. Still others are the shells of partly grown moon snails.

Some day you may visit an ancient shore in Virginia or Maryland. Though once a pretty beach, it now is a bank of clay and sand. Look at the gullies where rain water has run down. You will find the fossil shells of oysters, clams, and snails that lived millions of years ago. Some of them will be moon-snail shells. Then look carefully at your fossil clams. You will find that many show neat, round holes like those drilled by the moon snails on Holiday Shore.

Moon snails have lived in the sea for almost two hundred million years. Through all that time they have crawled in the sand, hunting snails and clams. During all those years they have been boring shells with their rough tongues and getting the good food inside with their sharp jaws.

Perhaps, while playing on Holiday Shore, you have found broken, leathery rings whose surfaces were covered with sand. Though you may not have known it, each of those rings held eggs laid by a mother moon snail.

You can tell Mother Moon Snail from Father only because she is larger than he. Her shell is rounded and smooth like his. She crawls as he does. She eats with the same table manners.

One warm summer day, Mother Moon Snail began to lay her eggs. Each time she laid a dozen or fifteen, she shut them up in a clear shiny capsule. She did this a great many times. Then she glued all the capsules into a ribbon that looked like crinkly celluloid. Next she covered one side of the ribbon with sand that she found near by. As she worked, she rolled the sheet around her body. In this way she shaped the sheet into a broad ring, like a broken bowl without any bottom.

After putting about half a million eggs into the capsules of that sandy ring, Mother Moon Snail left them lying on the sand and crawled off to hunt a mussel or a clam.

*Mother Moon Snail left about half a million eggs
in this sandy ring.*

For a month the egg-ring was washed here and there by the water. At last, when the eggs were ready to hatch, the ring broke into tiny bits. A great many baby snails hatched from the eggs that were in each bit, and they all went out to float in Holiday Bay.

These infant snails were so small they could be seen only with a microscope. Like little starfish, they drifted where waves and currents carried them. Some got close to rocks and were eaten by hungry barnacles and little animals that look like plants. Hundreds were sucked into the mouths of clams. Thousands were devoured by the purple mussels that lived near Holiday Point.

It is, as you may see, a good thing that Mother Moon Snail laid as many as the half million eggs or there would not have been enough babies left to grow into strong, hungry snails.

Thais, the Whelk

There are other snails on Holiday Shore that eat by boring holes in shells. One of them is called Thais, though her English name is whelk.

The whelk does not crawl in the sand. She lives on rocks and on Holiday Cliff. Twice a day the tide goes down and leaves her high and dry. But she does not mind. She just sits down, shuts her shell, and waits for the water to come again.

Do you think that all whelk shells of the same kind should look alike? Perhaps they should—but they don't. Some are wrinkled and some are almost smooth; some are sharp and others are blunt; some are white and others are yellow or even brown. A few have orange stripes on coarse ruffles of shell.

The whelk puts her eggs in little vases which she glues tightly to the rock. She puts about four hundred eggs in each vase. Even before they leave their vase the baby whelks are hungry. There is nothing else for food in the vase so some of the tiny whelks eat the others. By the time they are ready to leave the vase, there may not be more than a dozen to come out. They hide in cracks for a while until they grow big and strong enough to go hunting. Then they feed on mussel or barnacle meat, which they get by boring through the shells of these creatures.

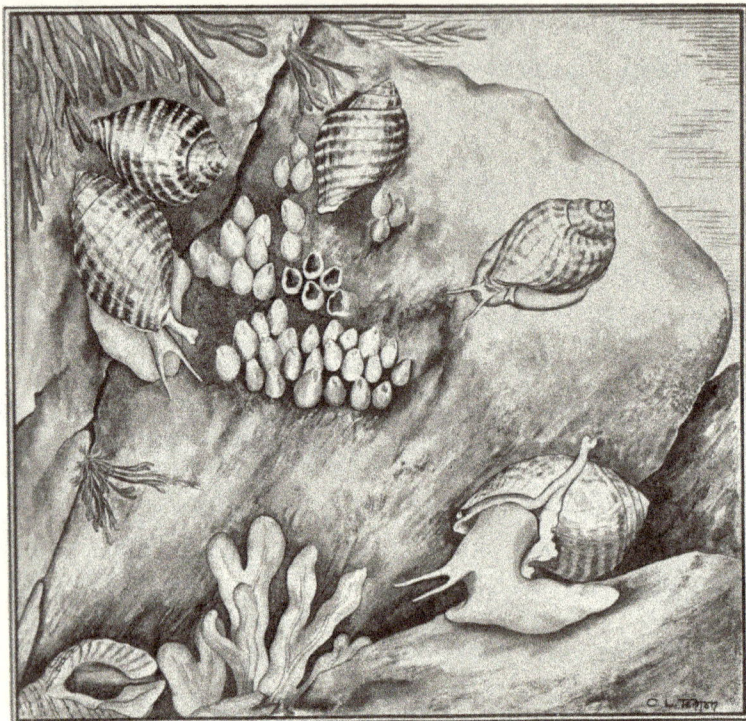

*Whelks put their eggs in vases
which they glue tightly to the rock.*

Periwinkles

Among the rocks and weeds where the whelks live there are thousands of snails called periwinkles. When the tide is high, they crawl here and there eating plants. When the tide is low, they hide in damp cracks or under the seaweeds if they can find such places.

But what happens to them if they cannot hide?

Look at that big bare rock. The sun has dried it

and made it warm, yet many periwinkles remain there. When the tide went out, each periwinkle fastened its shell to the rock with a bit of glue it made in its body. Then it tucked itself away in the shell and settled down for a nap until the next tide. If they really had to do so, they could sleep this way for days without touching water.

Periwinkles are the commonest snails on Holiday Shore.

Three kinds of periwinkles live on Holiday Shore. One is yellow. Another is green. The third and largest has a gray shell with dark stripes.

When white people first visited this part of the coast, they did not find any of these gray periwinkles. It was not until about sixty years ago that these snails entered Holiday Bay.

How did they get here? They crawled and drifted from Canada, where they probably were carried by ships from Europe. Each year they came farther and farther south. Now they are the commonest of all snails that dwell on Holiday Shore.

These periwinkles thrive best on rocks where the waves wash over them twice every day. Those that stay in muddy bays never are so large and smooth as the periwinkles of Holiday Shore.

The keyhole limpet, the largest of all hat-shells

Hat-Shells, or Limpets

What are these queer shells? They are oval and come to a low, sharp point. They are mottled with green, brown, and white. They cling very tightly to the rocks— so tightly that you cannot pull them off. If you find one, however, that has not been alarmed, perhaps you can lift it off by slipping a broad knife gently under its shell. Then, by turning it over, you will see the big flat foot by means of which it clings to the stone.

You will see the limpet's big flat foot.

These are hat-shells, or limpets. They do not live below low-tide level. It does them no harm to get dry. When the tide is high they crawl slowly about, eating tiny plants. When the tide begins to lower, or ebb, each limpet crawls back to the place from which it started.

43

Every limpet on Holiday Shore has its own special home.

There are different kinds of limpets. Some are small and rather smooth. Others have thick white shells that are rough. On the shore near Monterey, California, lives the largest limpet of all. It is three or four inches long, with a hole at its top instead of a peak. Its black body covers most of its shell, which is a very pretty light brown. People call it the keyhole limpet.

Ear-Shells

California's most famous sea-shells are those called abalones. You will often find washed up on the sandy shores empty shells that are a smooth greenish black outside and pearly inside.

The red abalone has a big rough shell. Its outer surface is a dark brick red. Old shells generally are covered with plants, moss animals, and tubes built by worms. From the number of things growing on their shells, you can tell that the red abalones live in deeper water than their smaller, black relatives do.

The peacock abalone is the largest of all. Outside it looks worn and weather-beaten; but its inside colors are brighter than those of any rainbow, as you can see when the body is taken from the shell. There shine blue, green, and red—like the colors on the feathers of a peacock's tail.

An abalone resembles one-half of a clam shell, yet it really belongs to the snail group. Look closely and

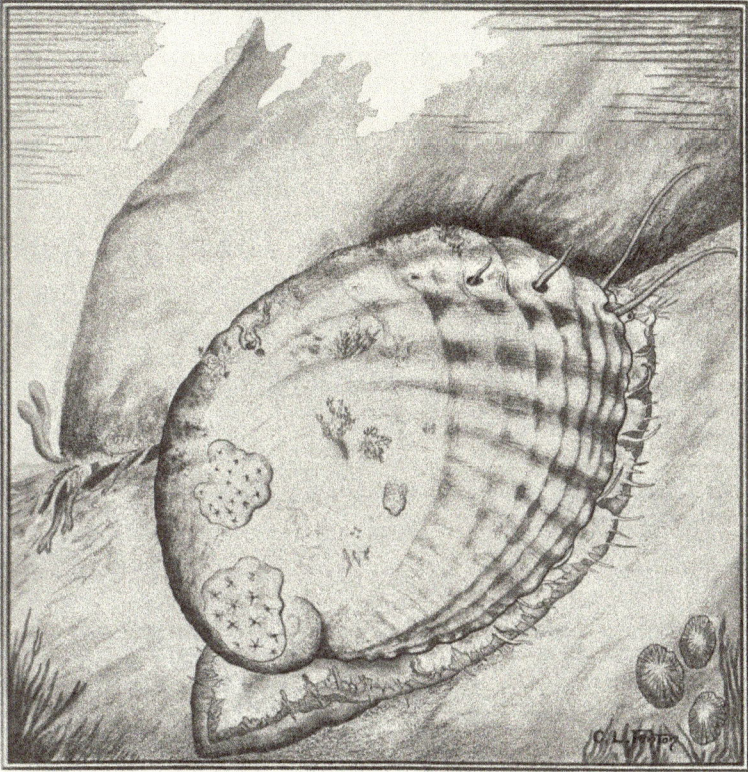

Moss animals, plants, and worms grow
on the shell of the red abalone.

you will see the coil in its shell. Like the limpet, the abalone crawls about eating plants, holding tightly to the rock if alarmed. Since its big muscles are good to eat, thousands of abalones are killed every year and sold in restaurants as "abalone steaks."

Shell-Less Snails

Do snails with clamlike shells seem queer? Then what do you think of snails that have no shells at all?

45

Two such creatures live on Holiday Shore. The larger of these is about an inch long. It looks much like a fat worm, mottled with white, yellow, and blue. You may not see it unless you hunt when the tide is very low, for it hides among the rocks.

Its smaller relative lives along rocks, seaweeds and eel-grass leaves. It is slender and pretty, with many waving plumes that are orange, purple, and blue. It lays eggs in long strings which it hangs from rocks and plants, or coils on flat stones.

Many relatives of these shell-less snails live on the Pacific coast. Some are small like those in the East, but others are large. One has very bright yellow colors, with

Sea hares of California

rich brown spots. It hides among seaweeds and rocks and lays long ribbons filled with eggs. If you catch one at just the right time, it will lay a beautiful salmon-pink ribbon of eggs in your aquarium.

When you wade in Southern California bays, you will see many big brown snails whose shells are so small they do not show. Their common name is sea hares, though they never act like rabbits, or hares. Instead of hopping, they crawl on the sand, leaving trails of slime behind them. Sometimes they open big flaps of skin and drift away with the tide. When they have gone far enough, they catch hold of eel-grass leaves to keep from floating out to sea.

Mother Loligo walked on her arms to the stone where she laid her eggs.

CHAPTER VI

LOLIGO'S TRICKS

LOLIGO and others like him often swim in the bay near Holiday Shore. If you go out in a boat, you can see them among the seaweeds.

Loligo is about eight inches long. He is shaped much like a tiny submarine and is pinkish, spotted with red and brown. Two big kite-shaped fins spread sidewise near his tail. His head is short, with round bright eyes. In front of his eyes are ten pointed arms. On each arm are many round suckers.

Surrounded by the arms, where you cannot see it, is a mouth with two sharp black beaks, and a tongue that is even rougher than the moon snail's tongue.

Loligo, who swims among the waving seaweeds, is a squid. Squids belong to a group of animals called mollusks, a name which means that their bodies are soft. So do clams, oysters, snails, and some others. If you like, you may call these soft-bodied animals cousins—but they really are not such close relatives as cousins. The group to which the squids belong are the only mollusks that swim. Most of the time they swim backward. How do you suppose they do that?

Under Loligo's chin is a slit. It connects with a big chamber in his body. When he fills the chamber with water, he shuts the slit. Then he squirts the water out through a tube that also lies under his chin. The force of the water as he squirts it out sends him backward through the bay.

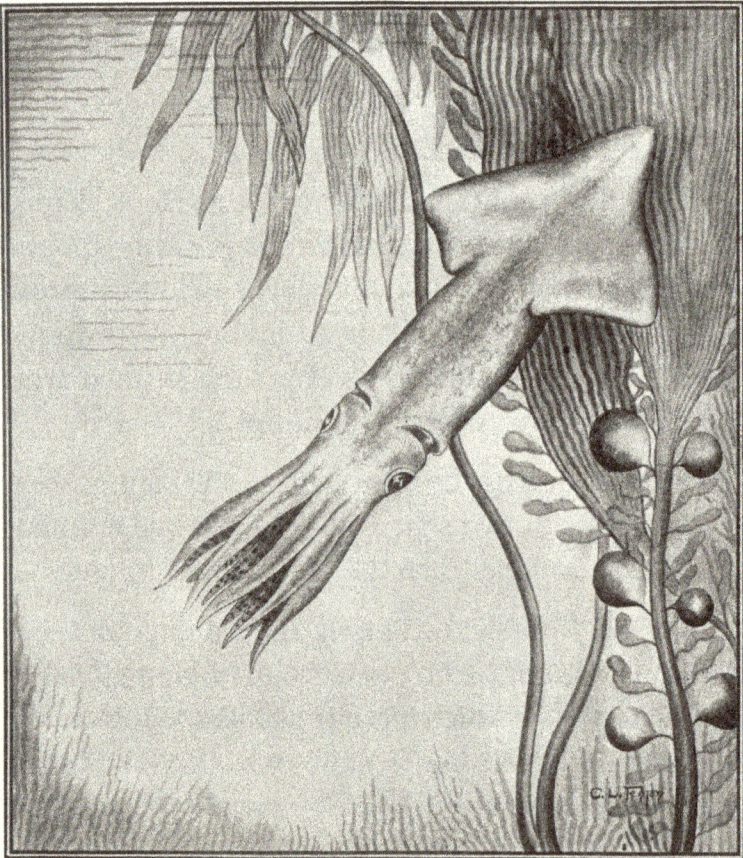

Loligo swam backward among the kelp and other seaweeds.

That is, it does when the tube points forward. If Loligo wants to turn, he twists the tube one way or another. He even can turn it so that it points toward his tail. Then he swims forward for a while.

Watch Loligo and those other two squids near him as some fish swim near. They all begin to twist their arms about. Their color fades to a pale whitish pink. Suddenly they begin to move, darting backward among the fish and turning from one side to the other. As they turn, they reach out with two long arms and try to catch the fish with their suckers.

The fish, which are mackerel, do their best to get away. Loligo misses the first and the second, but he catches the third with his two long arms. Then he bites pieces from it with his beak and tears these pieces with his rough tongue, before he finally swallows his food.

That second squid is a good hunter, but he does not take time to eat. Swimming about among the fish, he kills two or three by biting chunks out of their backs. Then he lets the dead fish drop to the bottom as he swims off to continue his hunt.

None of this meat is wasted. Crabs, snails, and jointed worms soon find it and enjoy the feast that the squid provided.

Meanwhile the mackerel that the squid was chasing have gone into shallow water—so shallow, indeed, that the squid does not venture to follow them. So after all his efforts, this greedy hunter has to go hungry.

The third squid was awkward or unlucky. He tried

51

his best to catch a fish, but every one swam away. At last he gave up the chase and settled down on the bottom of the bay. There his color is rapidly changing. He is being covered with buff and brown spots that look like sand. You must look carefully to see the waiting squid at all.

How do squids change color as they swim, hunt, or wait on the sand?

If you could put Loligo under a microscope, you would see that his skin contains hundreds of little cells called "color bodies." When these are open, the dark color in them spreads out and shows as spots. When they are closed the dark color does not show and the squid looks pinkish white. By closing and opening his color bodies, or cells, Loligo becomes pale pink or grows darker until he is purplish brown. He is sometimes so pale that you can hardly see him in clear water; and when he is hiding among seaweeds or waiting on the pebbles, he is so mottled that you may easily fail to see him there.

Loligo has another trick that he plays only when attacked. If a big, hungry fish tries to catch him, Loligo squirts out a cloud of ink and swims backward as fast as he can. By the time the fish gets his eyes out of the inky cloud, Loligo is far away, or hidden among seaweeds or rocks.

Soon he fills his ink bag again with black fluid he makes in his body. It is well to be prepared to escape from the next hunter that would like to eat the delicate flesh of the squid. Dangers make Loligo cautious, but they do not make him unhappy or drive him from

Holiday Bay. He even finds it such a pleasant place that he comes there with Mrs. Loligo when she is ready to lay her eggs.

One day in early summer, Mrs. Loligo squeezes a sticky ball out of the tube under her chin. First, she catches it with her arms. Then she swims backward for two or three minutes, rolling the ball between her arms until she has an object about four inches long shaped rather like a cigar.

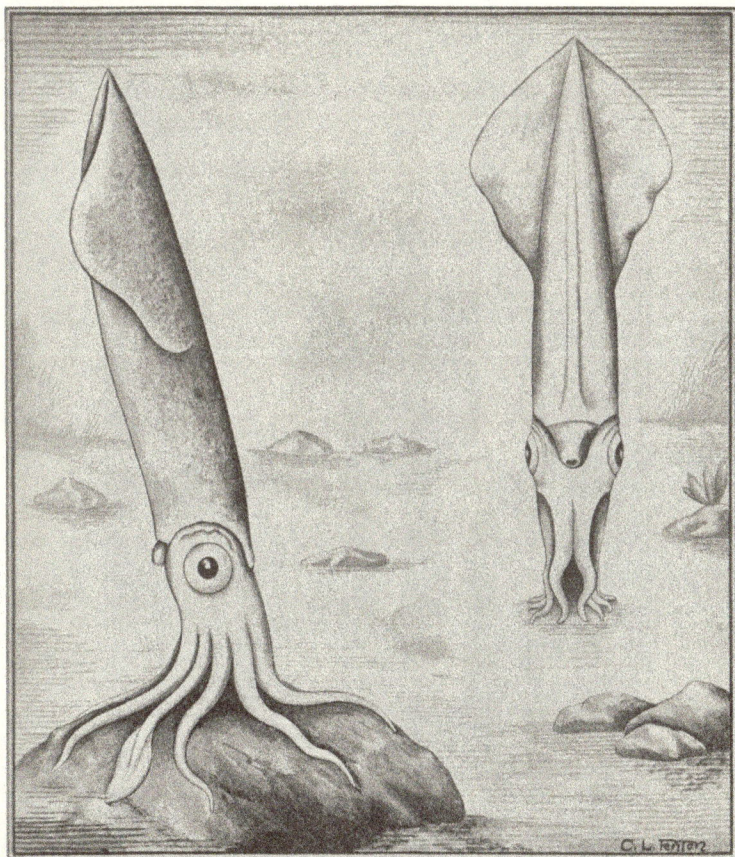

*Mother Loligo walked on her arms
to the stone where she laid her eggs.*

Suddenly she stops swimming and stands on her head. She walks about on the tips of her arms till she finds a satisfactory seaweed or stone. There she presses the sticky object firmly into place and gets ready to make another one.

That cigar-shaped roll holds several hundreds of Mrs. Loligo's eggs. Since she has several thousand eggs to lay she needs many such rolls to hold them all. So she forms one jellylike roll after another and fastens them in clumps which fishermen often call "sea mops."

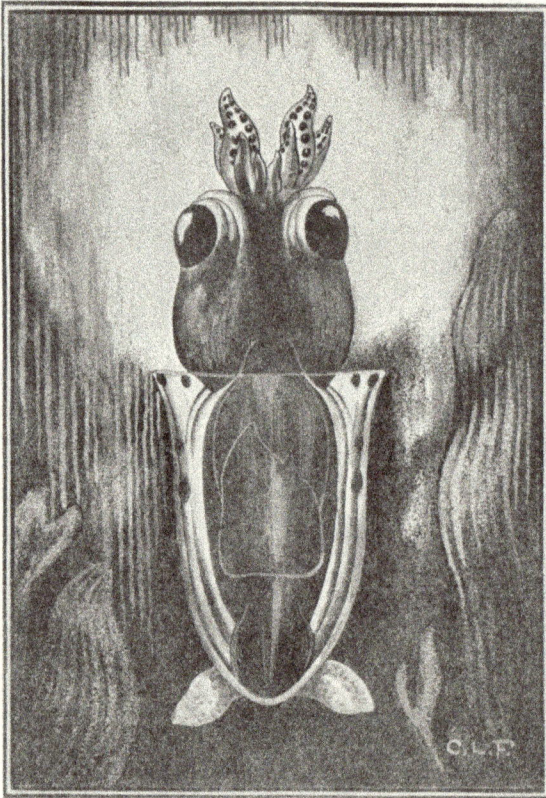

The baby squid has big eyes and short arms.

Each egg is small, round, and white. In a few weeks a baby squid hatches from it. His head is more than half as large as the rest of his body. His eyes are big and his arms are short.

His fins are two tiny flaps that stick backward near his tail. This youngster is less than a quarter of an inch long at first, but when he is a year old he will be as big as Mother or Father Loligo.

Sepia, the Cuttlefish

In the deepest tide pools we sometimes find one of Loligo's relatives. He is only five or six inches long, but his body is thicker than Loligo's. He has two narrow fins, one on each side, that run from his head to his tail. Eight of his arms, with suckers, are short and he uses them like feet. Two other arms are very long when they are stretched out, but he often carries them folded inside his head.

This is Sepia, the cuttlefish. Snails and clams carry their shells outside their bodies, but Sepia's shell is buried in his flesh, not far from his stubby tail. There it helps protect the soft inner parts of his body from being hurt by the bumps that he gets when swimming backward among the rocks.

Sepia also has a bag of ink that he squirts out to stop sea creatures from chasing him. Fishermen of ancient China and Rome caught cuttlefish and sold these bags to men who made the fluid into writing ink. Even now there is a dark "sepia" brown made from cuttlefish ink.

Perhaps you have some of it among your water-color paints.

Mother Sepia has her own way of laying eggs. She covers each one with a black coat, making it look like a little pointed grape. Then she fastens it to a frond of seaweed on a stalk that seems to be made of rubber. On this stalk the egg bobs to and fro until it is ready to hatch.

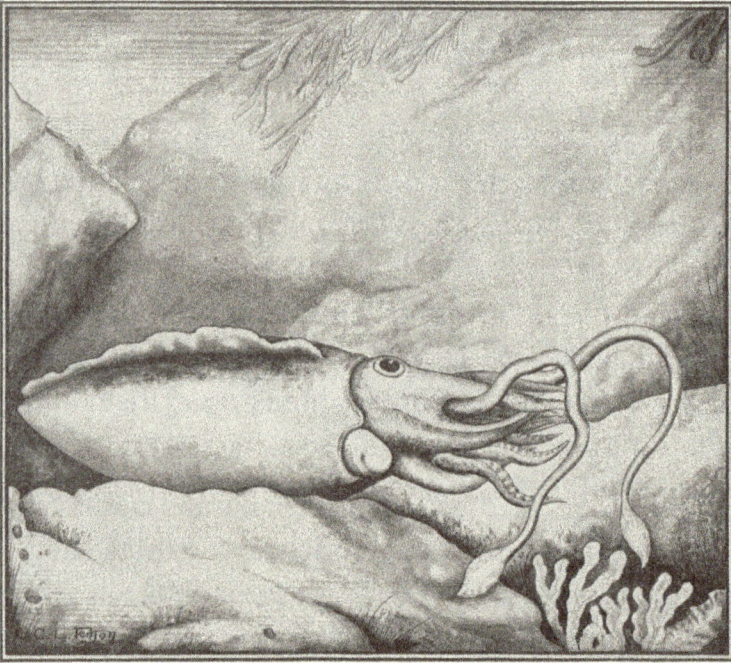

Sepia, the cuttlefish, among the rocks of a deep tide pool.

An Octopus

Have you read stories about the octopus, or devilfish, another of Loligo's relatives? Most of these stories speak of the octopus as if he were very fierce, but they are imaginary and do not give the facts. You need not be afraid if you are lucky enough to see an octopus along the rocks off Holiday Shore.

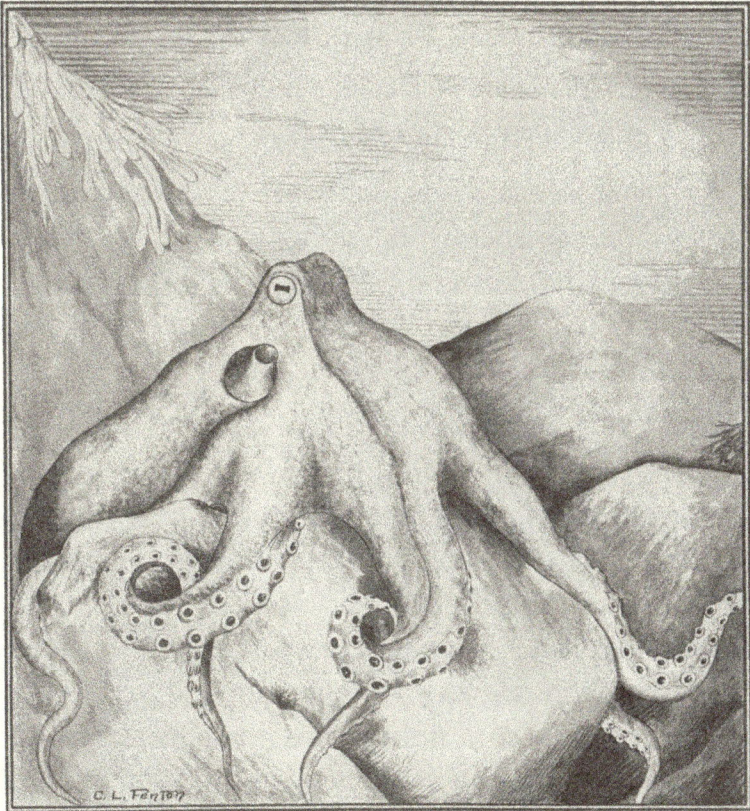

The octopus stretches and twists his arms.

The octopus has a soft, roundish body that is six or eight inches long. His head is short and his eyes are big. They seem to glare at you in a very savage manner, but the octopus will not hurt you. He is really a timid creature.

Instead of having ten arms, like the squid, the octopus has only eight. Watch this creature twist his long arms among the rocks, showing their big round suckers. Like the rest of his body, the arms are mottled with pink. But the octopus, like Loligo, can change his colors and become brownish or purple or nearly white. Even when he is not disturbed, the octopus twists and stretches his arms. He uses them when he crawls, pulling himself from rock to rock.

Do you see that crab among the rocks? The octopus sees it, too. He is crawling along until he gets above it. Suddenly he drops on the crab, holding it with his sucking arms while he bites through its hard shell. He is so hungry he does not even mind when the crab pinches one of his arms.

As soon as the octopus has finished his dinner of crab meat, take a stick and poke him a little—just to see what happens. At once he squirts out a cloud of ink, pulls his long arms from the rocks and swims backward through the water. Soon he hides himself among other rocks. If you should attempt to get him out, you would find that he hangs on tightly with his suckers. He will not try to bite you, but he holds firmly to the protecting rock. You may tug, if you like, but the octopus does not budge.

CHAPTER VII

KING LIMULUS

LIMULUS, the king crab, slept all winter on the quiet bottom of Holiday Bay, without moving a single claw. The water in the bay was very cold but that did not bother King Limulus.

When the autumn weather grew chilly, he did not need to look at a thermometer or worry about warming his home with a furnace fire. He made no attempt to keep warm. He just lay on the sand while his body grew numb with cold. By the time winter really came, he could not move or even feel.

During the fall, barnacles settled on his shell and little seaweeds began to grow. Before Christmas the King looked like a weedy rock lying on the bottom of the bay.

In time the spring sun warmed the dry earth. On land pussy willows bloomed. Robins came north again and began to build their nests. But the deep parts of Holiday Bay stayed cold, and the sleepy King did not awake.

The stiffness did not begin to come out of his joints

King Limulus stopped among the seaweed.

until some time after May day. First he stretched one leg, and then another, and so on until he had stretched all twelve of them. He lifted his long spinelike tail. Being able to move his body, he began to crawl toward shore. He came to a place where worms burrowed in the sand, and paused to dig them out and eat his first spring breakfast.

King Limulus had a strange way of eating. His mouth was on the under side of his head, between his six pairs of legs. First he pulled the worms out of the sand. Then he worked his legs to and fro, chewing the worms with sharp, hard spines. By the time he put the worms into his mouth, all he had to do was to swallow.

After the King had finished his meal, he crawled, half buried in the sand, toward the warm shallows near Holiday Shore. When he found a place where the sand was packed hard, he dug into it with his long sharp tail and used it to push himself along.

It took King Limulus several days to reach the shallows near the shore, where he stopped among the seaweeds and eel grass to warm himself and eat his dinner. Sun, shining through the water, heated his sandy lunch counter. In it were hundreds of pink and green burrowing worms. These made a feast fit for king crabs, and Limulus was not the only one of his kind who came to enjoy the treat. Indeed, in that sunny, watery lunch room, many members of his family met for the first time that spring. Among them may have been his father and some of his sons, but, if so, Limulus did not know one from another.

One day the King had rather a bad jolt. He was hunting worms in the shallows, as usual, while waves rolled up on Holiday Shore. One of them picked him up and threw him high on the beach.

It dropped him, top-side-down, and there he lay with his legs waving in the air! You need not feel sorry for him, however, because he was not nearly so helpless as he looked. He bent his shelled body and reached down with his tail. As soon as he could bend back far enough to stick the tip of his tail into the sand, he turned himself over with a twist and a flop. Then he crawled back to the bay as fast as his legs could go.

Only ten of his twelve legs really helped him travel. Those of the first pair were so short that they only wiggled about near his mouth. The last ones were extra long and ended in strong, paddle-shaped joints. The King used them to push sand aside when he burrowed into it for worms.

Behind his legs, the King had five pairs of broad plates. Under three of these were the gills with which he breathed air mixed with the water where he lived. The oxygen in the air, as you doubtless know, is as necessary to sea creatures as it is to land animals.

The gills with which fishes breathe are near their heads. So are the gills which baby frogs and toads use while they are tadpoles. But Limulus carried his gills just in front of his tail. Water animals, of different groups, have gills of different sorts and in different places. There are the infant dragon flies, for instance, which wear their gills in the tips of their tails.

While the King was turning himself right-side-up, the children playing near by came to watch him. They saw that his head was a big, horseshoe-shaped thing covered with a shiny, brownish-green shell. At each side, under a sharp point, was a glowing green eye. Two other eyes were placed near the front of his head. It is easy to overlook these for they seem to be merely two dark spots.

Fastened to the head by a wide joint was the broad

part of the body that covered the gills. On the edge of each side were six short sharp spines, and at the tip was the long spine that formed his useful tail.

Were the King's eyes of any use to him as he hurried back to the bay soon after he had righted himself?

No. He bumped into the stones that lay between him and the water and almost turned over on his back again. Even after he reached the water he swam thump into a rock and became tangled in some drifting seaweed. In spite of his two pairs of eyes, the King acted as if he were blind.

Queen Limulus meanwhile came to the bay and also began to hunt for worms. She looked like the King, except that she was bigger and broader and the legs of her second pair were shorter than his.

The King and the Queen seemed to pay no especial attention to each other, yet they did not go far apart. One morning, as the tide came in, they swam together as far up as they could and then crawled up on the beach.

There Queen Limulus dug a hole, while the King sat behind her and waited. In the hole she laid half a pint of eggs. Since each egg was very, very small it took about ten thousand of them to make that half pint. A great many eggs to leave in one nest!

Do you rather wish that the King and Queen had stayed beside the nest to guard it? They soon crawled away and never came back. But that was perfectly all right. There was not a thing they could have done if they had stayed. Those eggs were left where the sun could give them all the heat they needed. The warm sand that soon covered them was a satisfactory incubator.

Suppose we watch a single egg among the ten thousand Queen Limulus laid. Soon changes began to take place inside the clear, tough shell of the egg. In a week, traces of legs might be seen. Soon a head and body began to grow. In three weeks the baby could roll around inside the shell, but it made no attempt to get out.

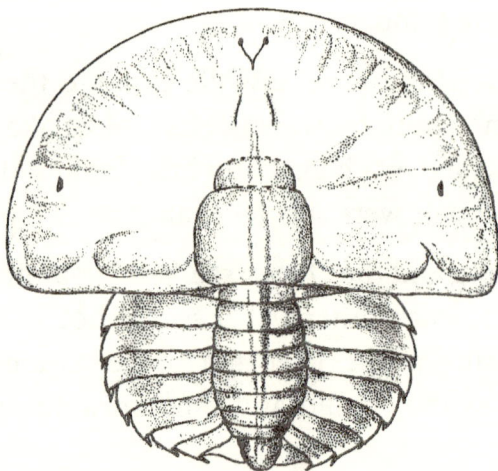

Baby Limulus just before hatching.

It was not until a month and a half after it was laid that the egg hatched. Then Baby Limulus went for a swim in Holiday Bay.

For about three weeks he swam here and there, dodging the mouths of hungry little hunters among the eel grass and rocks. Many of his brothers and sisters were caught and eaten by fish and sea anemones; but

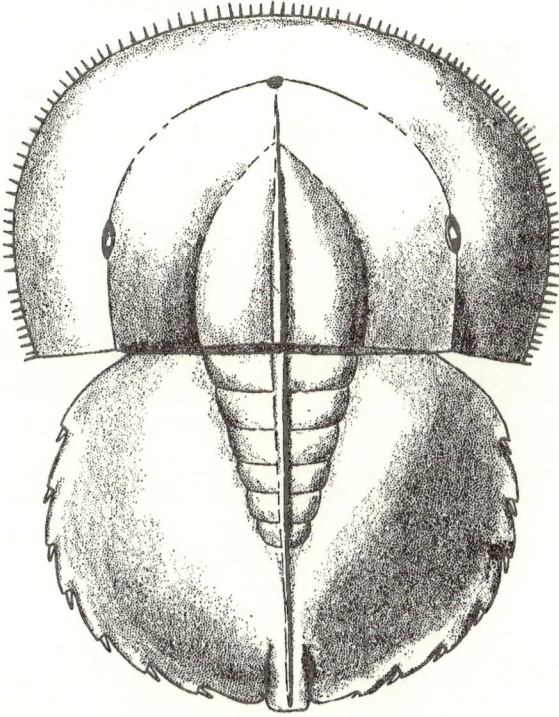

Baby Limulus just after hatching. He has not yet started to grow the long, sharp spine that will serve as his tail.

even so there seemed to be a good supply of infant king crabs in the bay.

Baby Limulus was rather a good hunter and caught and ate swimmers smaller than himself. As he grew, his tiny shell became too tight a fit for him; and one day he split it and appeared in a new and larger coat that had formed inside his first one. About that time he stopped his steady swimming and settled down in a sandy pool where the water stayed even when the tide was out.

This was his home for some time. He ate and grew

and shed his shell each time he needed a bigger one. By the time winter came, he was fast asleep in the sand. There he lay until the warm spring sun wakened him and made him feel spry enough to hunt for worms.

CHAPTER VIII

HERMITS AND OTHER CRABS

HERMIT was growing tired of his shell.

He had lived in this one all of three weeks, carrying it everywhere he went. Though he never traveled very far, he spent much of his time walking here and there under water that was not very deep. If, as sometimes happened, he got left on the shore by the tide, he rambled around in the first pool he came to. It did very well for a while.

Perhaps his body was feeling a bit squeezed as your foot does if your shoe is rather tight. Perhaps his shell had been scraped thin in places by being dragged over so many pebbles. Perhaps Hermit merely wanted a change.

However that may be, Hermit became interested when he saw a pretty moon-snail shell lying empty near him. He crawled up to it cautiously. He touched it with his antennæ, or feelers. It was smooth and whole. Then he rolled it over and over with his claws until it rattled on the stones. Next he pushed his large claw into it,

67

*Hermit tucked his body into the new, smooth shell
and walked away.*

making sure that nothing already lived in the place he wanted to use as a home.

At last he began to move. Catching the shell with one claw, he pulled his body out of the old shell and stuck it tail-first into the new one. For a moment he vanished inside. Then he came to the door and threw out some sand that had drifted into the empty shell. He had to do that several times before the shell was perfectly clean. Then he settled the soft part of his body into the whorls of his new house, stretched his legs through the doorway, and began to walk.

Soon Hermit quickened his pace. He was actually running, bumping his shell on pebbles, and scrambling over bits of sea lettuce. He waved his antennæ to and fro and wriggled the tiny feet near his mouth. Hermit was excited. He sensed that there was good food near by. He could not see it. He could not smell as you can. But he could catch a taste of food even while he was some little distance away. So he hurried along on the four long, slender, jointed legs he used for traveling, in an attempt to reach the food in time.

At the very edge of Holiday Shore, Hermit found his picnic dinner. It was a clam served on a half-shell. A man, digging in the sand, had broken its shell with his sharp spade. He threw it into the shallow water so that animals might find it there and have a meal.

How they did rush to this feast! First some wriggling green worms arrived from a very near spot. They tore bits of meat from the clam with their sharp, hook-shaped jaws. They squirmed and pushed with their many legs, trying to keep their greedy neighbors away.

Next came half a dozen little, rough snails that had been crawling rather near. They crowded in among the worms to get their share of clam meat. Then came the hungry Hermit in his new, smooth shell.

His table manners were all right for a hermit crab but no one could call them polite. He pushed the snails and worms aside. With his largest claw he tore off a piece of meat that was much too large for his little mouth. Instead of getting out of the way of the other picnickers, he sat next the clam and tore his piece into strips small enough for his jaws to take care of.

He ate so very fast that his stomach was soon full. Yet he still held a piece of meat. It was quite too good to throw away. Holding it in the small legs near his mouth, he walked slowly into deeper water. Twice he stopped and tried to eat, but his mouth was so full that he could not cram in another crumb. Finally he let the meat drop and sat down in the shade of a stone.

Hermit was careful to keep himself clean. Now that he had had a good meal, he took time for his toilet.

For almost an hour Hermit sat by the stone, cleaning his hard, spiny skin. He used his large right claw and then his left. He scraped and pulled tiny plants from his back and legs. He polished his long, jointed antennæ and the two stalks that held his eyes.

Hermit was not wasting time when he worked so hard to get himself clean. If he had not pulled those tiny plants off, they would have grown into long streamers of seaweeds. Then they would have bothered him when he crawled, and would have prevented him from drawing back into his shell when something dangerous came near. It would have been hard for him to escape some creature that was hungry for crab meat.

When he was shiny and clean, Hermit felt ready for more vigorous exercise. A fight would do! He walked slowly about the bay until he met another hermit crab who was also eager to fight.

Hermit stopped and waved his claws. The other crab stopped and waved his. Then they ran toward each other, their shells rattling on the stones. They hit each other with their claws; pinched feelers and legs; pulled, rolled, and wrestled among the seaweeds. Once Hermit was on top, pulling at the other crab's legs. In a moment his opponent got a firm hold and threw him head-over-heels. Then Hermit pinched one of the other's eye stalks, and the crabs pulled apart to get new holds.

It was then that Hermit made his mistake. In backing off to get a new, fierce run, he rolled backward over a stone. The thump on his shell startled him so much that he did not guard against attack.

At once his opponent ran up, reached inside Hermit's shell house, caught one of his tender hind legs, and began to pull. After three or four jerks, Hermit let go his hold on his protecting shell and was thrown out among the seaweeds.

Hermit was now in real danger. If one of his legs had been pulled off that would not have mattered too much. He could have grown a new one when he next shed his skin. But now the whole delicate part of his body was bare. If his thin, tender skin were injured, he probably would die. That was why it had been important for him to brush all the gritty sand out of the shell before he moved into it. And now he had lost that shell!

However, you need not worry about Hermit. The other crab did not try to hurt him. Instead, he turned his attention at once to the empty shell. He looked it over and felt it with his claws and antennæ. Then he took a firm hold of it and with a few swift motions moved out of his own snail shell into Hermit's.

Why did he make this change? Nobody knows. His own shell was just as good as the one he took away from Hermit. In fact, it was a better fit for he was larger than Hermit, and he looked very crowded indeed as he squeezed himself into Hermit's shell.

Do you suppose that when he had made his change, the crab left his deserted shell for Hermit? Well, he did not. That would have been a fair trade but it would not have been a crablike thing to do. You may recall that Hermit earlier in the day had taken more meat than he could eat and greedily carried it away. Just now the victor crab did not lose interest in his old shell, although he no longer needed it. He guarded this empty shell, waving his big claws fiercely when Hermit tried to get near it.

Thus they sat for more than half an hour. Hermit hid his bare body in a crack between two rocks. Each time he reached for the empty shell, the other crab frightened him back.

While they were quarreling, a third crab came near, waving his claws in a signal to fight. Hermit's opponent ran to attack. Here was Hermit's chance. He came at once out of the crack and climbed into the empty shell for which he had waited so long.

What do you suppose he did then? Instead of slipping quietly away, he ran to the two quarreling crabs and began to take a hand in their fight!

During this combat, no one was pulled from his shell. The fighters wrestled and tumbled about until suddenly one of them ran away. Then the others stopped struggling and walked off as if not a thing had happened.

As a matter of fact nothing unusual had happened. Indeed, Hermit seemed to enjoy wrestling matches, and they were very common affairs. Perhaps fighting was his way of getting part of his daily exercise.

Little Green Crab and Rock Crab

Here comes another boxer—the little green crab that dwells among rocks. He does not need a snail shell to protect him, for his whole body is covered with hard, tough skin that makes a shell of his own. He has two pinching claws and eight other legs. He threatens you when you pick him up, and tries his best to nip your fingers the moment you put him down.

Watch him run sidewise to the nearest crack between two rocks. Drop him into a pool and he will

Two green crabs wave their claws at each other
ready to start a fight.

find some place there to hide. Soon, however, he will be out again ready to meet another green crab. Both will wave their claws and scramble up to attack. Like Hermit, they will push and pinch until they are tired. Then they will sidle off to enjoy their dinners.

What do they eat? Watch one of the green crabs as he crawls up to a frond of sea lettuce. He picks off little bits with his claws and puts them daintily into his mouth. Meanwhile his neighbor finds an old shell, covered with a filmy growth of plants. He turns it over

74

slowly with one claw, picking off pieces which he eats in the same manner as the other crab nibbles sea lettuce.

In that tide pool over there is still another crab. His shell is yellowish spotted with brown. It is short and very wide, and his legs are fringed with hairs. He is twice as big as the little green crab and his pincer claws are twice as strong.

This is the rock crab. If you watch as you walk along Holiday Shore, you may find some of his brothers buried up to their eyes in sand, for they often rest in a sandy bed when they are not eating plants and soft animals in the tide pools.

A crab does not drag its tail behind the rest of its body where you can see it as the crab walks. It curls its tail under its body, making an armored pouch. In this pouch Mother Crab fastens her eggs. They hatch into little swimming animals less than one-tenth of an inch long. They have big dark eyes and long tails. They swim by jerking jointed affairs that some day will form parts of their mouths.

As a baby crab grows, its legs appear just in front of the tail. Each time the baby outgrows its tail, it crawls out of its cover with a new one. Then one day the little creature seems to have convulsions. It is not really ill, however. It is merely molting by crawling out of its skin in a more crablike shape. Its eyes still are very large, but its tail is now small and its first pair of legs have tiny pincers at their tips.

After a few days, the baby sheds its skin once more and begins to crawl instead of swim. After this it changes shells only twice a year until it becomes a full-grown crab. Then it must keep the same shell as long as it lives. If you hunt among the tide pools, you will find some very old crabs. You can tell which they are because plants and barnacles have grown on them since they got their last new coat.

Western Crabs

Does the shore where you like to go for holidays lie on the Pacific coast? If it does, you will not find rock crabs or their little, fighting, green relatives.

When you look in cracks and under bunches of seaweed, you will find many small purple crabs whose shells are spotted with green. You may wade in salt-water sloughs and find hundreds of little yellow crabs that run sidewise across the mud and try to pinch your fingers. If you attempt to pick them up, they will run away, just as the crabs do in New England.

You will also find many hermit crabs on a Western shore. Some of them that are very small live in little red or green shells that they find for their shelters. Others are bigger than most of the hermits living on the Atlantic coast. Some have their legs, claws, and even their heads covered with sharp hairs or spines. These hermits are striped with red, blue, and white, and are very pretty as they crawl about in brightly colored shells.

CHAPTER IX

WAITING BARNACLES
AND WORMS

THE tide was rising on Holiday Shore. As it covered the cobbles and the foot of the cliff, millions of little white shells opened to capture floating food.

The hungry creatures inside these shells were barnacles. Now, though barnacles have shells that open and shut, they are not related to clams. Strange as it may seem, their nearest relatives are crabs. When a barnacle is young, it swims in the water, just as a baby crab does.

If you dip water in a very fine net, you may catch some baby barnacles. At first they are tiny, colorless things floating about the bay. Naturally, many of them float into the mouths of hungry animals near shore; but as many live to grow up as there seems to be room for.

A very young barnacle has a three-cornered shell, one eye, and three pairs of jointed bristly legs. Growing older, he becomes oval in shape, while his shell has two halves like that of a clam. Next, the infant gets six pairs of feet, with which he swims rapidly in the bay. When the baby barnacle becomes tired, he rests on a rock.

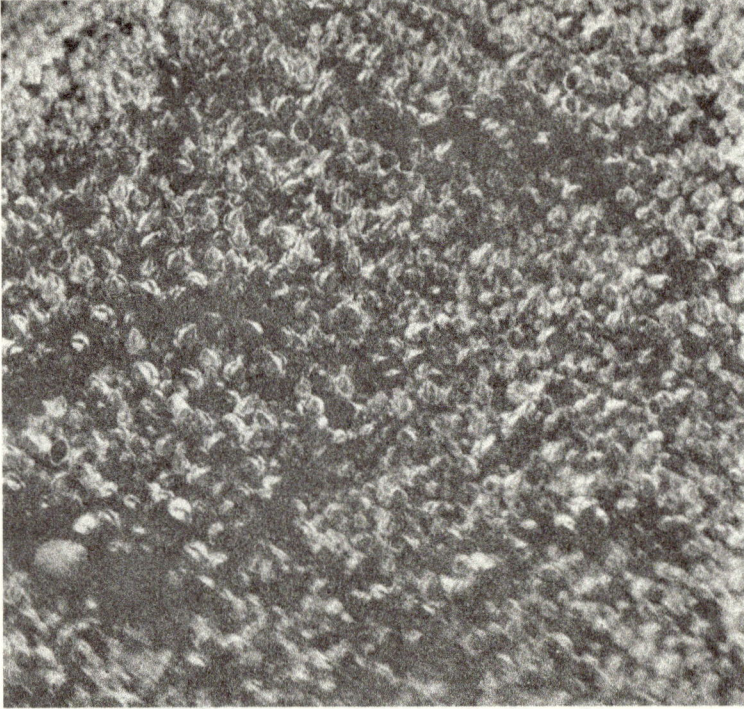

There are millions of barnacles on the rocks of Holiday Shore.

He holds himself to it by antennæ, or feelers, that grow from his small, round head.

As the barnacle grows, he becomes less and less active. Finally he settles headfirst on a rock and gives up swimming altogether.

When the barnacle next sheds his skin, he gets a new kind of cover. On it are two small shells that open upward. Around them are six little pieces that spread and fasten to the rock. They soon become hard plates of lime that protect the soft body inside.

In time the barnacle's shell becomes higher than it

is wide. It is shaped somewhat like a tiny volcano with two lids for the opening at its top.

After the barnacle you see over there, for example, started to live with his head fastened to the rock, he could not, of course, use his legs for swimming. Instead, he spread them out like the parts of a fan which waved through the water and back into the shell. Hour after hour he kept his legs moving, bringing currents of water to the mouth inside the strong white shell.

The barnacles kept their legs moving hour after hour.

What did the barnacle get from the water? Many tiny bubbles of air to breathe, and food to eat. Exceedingly small plants and animals that floated near were the things he had for a meal. Baby clams, a starfish, and barnacles, that were so young they were drifting about in the water, were a part of his diet.

What else did he do? Very little. He could not go away for a swim, since his shell was tightly grown to the rock. Neither could he crawl into a cool damp crack when the tide went out. Of course, if he lived in a tide pool, it made no difference to him whether the tide was in or out, for there was always water in the pool and he simply kept on breathing and eating. But his neighbors who lived on the open rocks had to close their shells to hold the moisture inside until the tide returned. If rain fell between tides, these exposed barnacles had another reason for closing their shells. It was important to keep the rain out, for a dose of fresh water can kill most barnacles.

Children who visit tide pools in Quebec and England see barnacles of the same sort as those that may be found by millions covering the rocks of Holiday Shore.

The barnacles on rocks such as Holiday Cliff, where the tide leaves them uncovered for rather long times twice every day, do not live to be old. They die when they get to be two years old, and their shells break up and wash away. On some shores you will find white lime sand that is made of broken barnacle shells.

Those that live in deep water grow bigger, heavily wrinkled shells, and probably live several years.

Goose Barnacles

Have you ever heard sailors tell about goose barnacles that fasten themselves to ships? They also live on wharf piles and rocks. If you take a boat along Holiday Cliff, you will find some of them on the point where waves roll in from the open ocean far beyond Holiday Bay.

Their name, goose barnacles, comes from a queer old legend. People once thought these barnacles grew on trees and hatched into tiny geese of some sort. In the year 1597 a man published a book in which he said that he had seen this happen!

Really, of course, goose barnacles live in the sea and their eggs hatch baby barnacles. Those babies swim and drift until they are old enough to settle down on their heads. But instead of fastening their shells to the rock, they grow long leathery stalks on top of which are their bodies and shells.

You will notice these stalks as soon as you see the barnacles. Some of them are four inches long, twisting and bending with every wave. The shells are smooth and bluish white, set in brown and orange flesh. As you watch, the legs spread out like jointed plumes to bring in currents of water holding air and food.

Because they can live on the bottoms of ships, goose barnacles travel all over the world. While traveling, they lay their eggs. The baby barnacles hatch, grow, and settle down wherever they happen to be. So it happens that goose barnacles like those on Holiday Point live on both shores of the Atlantic, Pacific, and Indian Oceans; in the Gulf of Mexico, and in the Mediterranean Sea.

Goose barnacles put out their legs to catch food.

Tube Worms

Among the barnacles on Holiday Shore are many little creatures that live in tubes. Some of these tubes are slender and white, twisting about on clams or rocks. Other white tubes are coiled and shaped like shells of certain snails. These may be found on stones or clinging to seaweeds that grow in the bay and in sheltered tide pools.

Though they look so much like the houses of snails, these tiny shells really belong to worms. Put some of them in a dish of sea water and watch them through a magnifying glass if you wish to see the worms that live in them.

Tube worms in snail-like shells,
seen through magnifying glass.

You will need to wait a while, for these worms are timid, and at first their shells will be tightly closed by little plugs of hard flesh. But as soon as the water in the dish becomes quiet, and the worms get over the scare you gave them when you moved them, they will open their shells and begin to eat. First the plug is pushed out to one side; then you will see a ring of yellow or red plumes.

Those plumes really are the gills through which the worm breathes, but they also get his meals for him. Watch them as they bend and twist, sending currents of water with food into his mouth. Though the tube worm is not related to his barnacle neighbors, he eats in much the same way.

Worms that build the long twisted tubes are much larger than those with snail-shaped shells that stay on the seaweeds. Look in almost any tide pool; you will see their pretty red gills waving like feathers at the mouths of their shells. That is, you will if you are quiet enough. Otherwise every worm in the pool will pull itself back into its home.

When these tube worms were very, very young, they drifted in Holiday Bay as did so many others of the babies of the bay. Those of them that found their way settled down on the rocks of Holiday Shore, when they were old enough to do so.

There they began to make tubes of lime, fastened tightly to shells or stones. As they grew, they added more lime to their tubes, but they did not build them straight. So now their homes twist and coil, or even wind around one another. You might guess from their shapes that they belonged to wriggly worms, even if you could not see the builders.

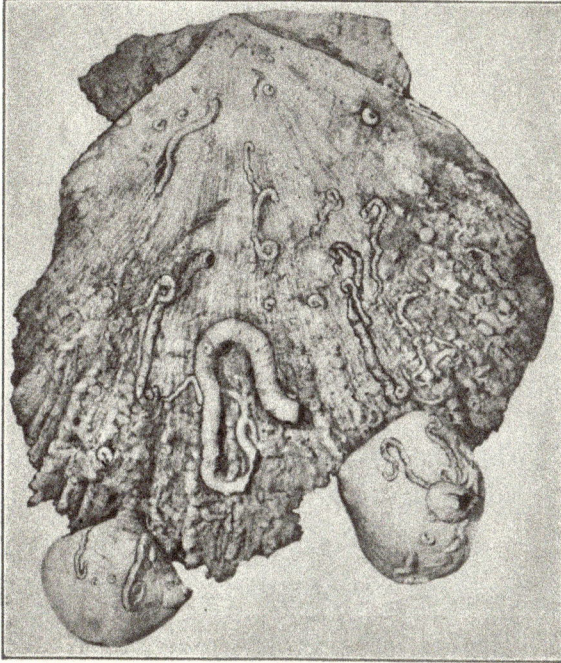

The tubes of these worms twist and coil.

CHAPTER X

NESTING TIME
AMONG THE FISHES

Father Stickleback

IT WAS early summer and Father Stickleback darted about in his gayest suit. His cheeks and throat were gleaming red and his eyes shone like bluish-green gems. Most of his body was shiny green above and silvery underneath.

Unlike many fishes, Father Stickleback had no scales, but he did wear a row of bony plates along each side. These plates seemed like strips of enamel, and you may call them his coat of mail, if you like. Along the middle of his back was a row of stickles, or daggerlike spines. His jaws were short, though strong, and his teeth were sharp.

Father Stickleback built a nest. He brought bits of seaweed and fastened them to the lower stems of sea plants with tough elastic fibers, or threads.

The material for these fibers was made in a special gland in his body. While inside the gland the material was a liquid, but as soon as the fish spun it into the water it hardened to a fiber that he could use in building his nest.

Father Stickleback's building material may remind you of the silk that caterpillars and spiders make in glands in their bodies. Silk, too, is a liquid while inside the glands, and it hardens to a fiber as it is spun and touches air.

Father Stickleback guards his nest.

The little builder shaped his nest like a tiny muff. He made the inside smooth by swimming along the wall and pressing against it with his body. There were two round doorways just the right size for sticklebacks to use.

After finishing this very good nest, inside and out, Father Stickleback rushed off to invite a Mother Stickleback to lay her eggs in it. He swam beside her to show her the way. As soon as she had placed her eggs on the floor and had gone out through one doorway, Father Stickleback went in at the other and put some milt over them. Fish eggs, as you may know, need milt to make them grow just as plant seeds need pollen.

The nest was not yet nearly full of eggs. What could be done with all that extra room? It was not wasted. Father Stickleback hurried away and invited other Mother Sticklebacks to put their eggs there, too. So they came with him, one at a time, until the little nursery was filled with eggs almost to the doorways.

Father Stickleback waited near the home he had built, guarding it from snails and other intruders. When the eggs were about ready to hatch, he went into the nest and moved clumps of them, lifting them with his mouth and letting the water flow freely among them.

The eggs did not all hatch the same day. Some of Father Stickleback's sons and daughters were two or three days old before the youngest of the fry, or baby fish, were hatched. After moving about inside the nest for a number of hours, the older babies went to the doorway. The watery world looked pleasant as far as they could see, and after a little wait one of them slipped outside for a swim. He did not go far. Father Stickleback hastened after the tiny runaway, picked him up in his mouth, and took him back inside his home before he let him go. Soon another venturesome baby started out and had to be brought back in the same way. One after another those youngsters kept their father busy, but all the while he was careful and gentle. In all his hurry he did not bite one of them.

Within a few days, however, the last of the eggs were hatched and the whole family of little Sticklebacks, forty or fifty in number, were eager to leave their crowded nursery. So out they swam and this time their father did not take them back. He went with his brood, guiding the little fry from place to place. He protected them by swimming with them and keeping hungry creatures away.

This little father is only about three inches long and you might think to glance at him that it would be all he could do to take care of himself. He is not, however, so helpless as you may suppose from his size. He is not at all timid. He is brave enough to bite pieces from the fins of really large fish. Indeed, he can fight quite fiercely if necessary.

Father Hippo Campus

While the Sticklebacks are moving swiftly about the bay they often pass Hippo Campus, a little fish who looks so much like a horse that he is called "Sea Horse" for one of his names. He has no scales on his body, but he is protected by bony plates that cover him from the top of his head to the tip of his tail.

Yes, there he goes now swimming with his body held erect—head up and tail down. When he comes to rest he is likely to grasp the stem of some sea plant with his finless, coiled tail and hang head down. In this position does the queer little fish make you think of a monkey swinging from a branch by his grasping tail?

Father Sea Horse guarding young sea horses

Hippo Campus does not become dizzy as he rests in this way. He does not suffer from a rush of blood to the head. He is perfectly comfortable. He looks about him and sees Mother Sea Horse hanging head down with her tail twisted around the stem of a neighboring plant.

Since it is time for Mother Sea Horse to lay her eggs, she drops them into the water. They sink to the sand beneath her and she does not need to pay any attention to them at all. Father Hippo Campus untwists his tail from the plant stem and goes down after the eggs. He picks them up and puts them into a little egg pouch on the under side of his tail. Then he closes the opening with a special sort of glue he has. The father fish hangs himself up again by his tail in a place where the sun shines on him and warms the eggs in the pouch. When it is time, the young hatch from the eggs and find themselves wriggling inside the dark, closed pouch. There they stay until they grow so strong that they can wriggle hard enough to punch an opening in the side of the egg pouch. Then out go the fry—a whole herd of tiny sea horses.

Journeys to Fresh Water

Ocean sticklebacks and sea horses do not travel far at nesting time. They do not leave sea water to spawn (lay their eggs). Their young, like those of many other fish, thrive in salt water. There are fish, however, that migrate, or travel, to fresh water before they spawn. The young, or fry, of such fish, start their lives in lakes or streams and seek the ocean when they need a change.

These migrants are not regular neighbors of the sea horses and sticklebacks. They are visitors from farther off the coast that enter Holiday Cove during their journeys. For a few weeks each spring they use the cove for a gathering place through which they pass on their way to Holiday Stream and Holiday River.

There are the smelts, for instance. They are most numerous during the flood tide of the May moon. These fish migrate in crowds, called schools, as far as the high tide reaches, and glue their eggs to stones where the fresh water of Holiday Stream will flow over them when the tide goes out. The father and mother smelts return to the sea with the ebbing tide. Their spawning trip is a short one.

The alewives, too, come hurrying into the cove every spring. They are members of the Herring Family, as you might guess from the shape of them. They go to the foot of the falls that pour out of Holiday Stream into the cove. In their eagerness to reach the fresh water they push together so tightly that not even little Father Stickleback could find room to slip between them. The dark fins on their backs show above the water like tiny sails. There they wait until the tide comes in and lifts them higher and higher, and then at last they can climb over the top of the falls and make their way up stream.

It is exciting to see the alewives scrambling over the top rocks of the little falls in the stream, but it is even more thrilling to watch the salmon in Holiday River. These spring migrants leave the ocean by way of the cove and swim to the rapids at the base of the falls in the river. There these leapers jump out of the water and over the rocks from place to place until they reach the river above the falls. Then they travel until they come to a quiet lake.

After all their rush to get into fresh water in the spring, it is not until late fall that the mother salmon lay their eggs and the fathers cover them with milt. There in the sand near the edge of the lake the eggs remain in cold storage all winter. When the ice above them melts and the water around them is warmed by the sun in the

Atlantic salmon on their spring journey

spring, the eggs hatch. The salmon fry live for a while in the lake and then, when they are old enough, they travel slowly down the river to the cove, and so on to the waters of the coast.

Of course Father Stickleback and Father Hippo Campus do not know that all the young smelts and alewives and salmon that come down stream and visit the cove for a while are the sons and daughters of the parent fish that hurry into the cove in the springtime. These little stay-at-homes know nothing at all of the habits of migrants that leave the sea and seek fresh water for the spawning season.

CHAPTER XI

EELS AND LAMPER EELS

Voyages of the Eels

CERTAINLY neither Stickleback nor Hippo Campus knows where the old eels are going when they pass through the cove on their way from the fresh-water in which they grew up to seek in the far sea places to leave their eggs. Yet the eels and their manners are worth knowing, for they are the most famous of all migrating fish. They depart in crowds from rivers that empty into the Atlantic Ocean and gather in the deep water between Bermuda and the Leeward Islands.

There the father and mother eels spend their spawning season. So the young eels hatch from their eggs in that far-distant place. Do you suppose they stay there? They do not. They start in a northerly and westward direction while they are still very young. After living about a year in the sea, they enter the rivers the old eels left so long before. How do they find their way? Nobody really knows.

If you poke about among small plants near the

shore, you are quite likely to find one of these little eels on his way to Holiday River. You may call him "Elver" if you like.

Elver is about two and a quarter inches long by the time he reaches the shore. He is colorless and as clear as glass, and his body is slender and round.

Before Elver reached Holiday River,
his body had become slender.

He was not at all like that when he started on his long sea voyage. Indeed, during most of his journey, the baby eel had much the shape of the blade of a small pocketknife. He was as thin as a leaf. If you had placed his flat little body on this page you could have seen the black letters through it almost as easily as you can see them through a piece of clear glass.

Baby eels are thin and flat.

After you say good-by to Elver while he is wriggling slowly toward the mouth of the river, it will be several years (perhaps five or six) before he returns to the shore. If you and Hippo Campus see him then, he will be on his way, with a crowd of other eels, to the distant place beyond Bermuda where he was born.

"Lamprel" and "Agnatha"

Lamprel is not really a fish, as an eel is. He is a sea lamprey. However, his smooth body is almost as slippery as an eel's and he looks so much like an eel that people call him "lamper eel" or "lamprel."

Lampreys spend most of their lives in sea water, and like certain fish we have mentioned, they migrate to fresh water for their nesting season. You and Hippo

Eels and sea lampreys

Campus are quite likely to meet them at Holiday Shore in the spring of the year. Perhaps, then, you may wish to be introduced to Lamprel and learn how to tell him from an eel. That is more, by the way, than some people know.

Lamprel has no coat of scales on his naked, slimy body, but a lack of scales would not help you tell him from an eel, because an eel's scales are so tiny and so hidden in its skin that you would not notice them at all.

But Lamprel has no bones—and who ever heard of a boneless fish? Instead of a bony skeleton, Lamprel has only strong gristle for the firmer parts of his body. He has a nose with only one nostril. Instead of having gills, as a fish has, he has a row of seven slits on each side of his neck. Each slit opens into a little bag called a gill pocket.

This strange creature has plenty of teeth—nearly one hundred and fifty of them, in fact. They are hard, sharp, cone-shaped teeth, more like tiny pieces of horn than bone. Lamprel has no jaws to which they can be attached, so he wears them fastened to the inside of his mouth and on his tongue. He can neither bite nor chew, but he can cling to his food with his sucking mouth and scrape it to shreds with his many teeth.

Lamprel's sucking habits are useful when he travels or rests, as well as at mealtime. He cannot swim against a current of water as a fish can, for he has no paired fins or limbs of any other kind. He moves about very well without limbs, however. He can take a short plunge ahead even in a strong current, and then catch hold of a stone with his mouth and cling to it until he is ready to take another plunge.

Knowing how Lamprel anchors himself to stones, you may not be surprised to learn that one name for a lamprey is "stone sucker."

As likely as not, you may find Lamprel sucking a stone near Holiday Shore when he is about to start on his trip into fresh water to seek his nesting site. A crowd of other lampreys will be keeping him company.

This will be in May, and while you watch the resting lampreys, schools of smelts and thousands of alewives may hurry past.

Slowly but surely—that is the way the lampreys travel. Even when they come to the falls over which the salmon went with such violent leaps, Lamprel and his companions take their time. It is now the darkest part of the night, but the lampreys are not discouraged. They need no light by which to find their way. They climb by plunging and clinging, little by little, until at last they reach the top.

Going over the falls is the hardest part of Lamprel's journey. One night, soon after that, a large fish swims near enough so that Lamprel fastens his mouth to the fish's side. As the fish is going up stream, Lamprel keeps his hold and rides for several miles.

When the migrating lampreys reach a rapid stream that empties into Holiday River they travel up that. On their way they meet some eels that will linger there until their migration time comes a few months later. Lamprel and the other father lampreys go a little ahead of the mother lampreys and pick out places for the nests. Each selects a rather shallow spot with a sandy bottom and plenty of pebbles.

By the time Lamprel has cleared the pebbles away from the sand where his nest is to be, a mother lamprey arrives and begins to help him. You may call her Agnatha, if you like. That name is an old word meaning "without jaws."

The current of the stream is so swift that the nest

needs to be protected from it. Agnatha and Lamprel do this by piling stones at the edge of the nest to make a breakwater on the up-side of the nest and a little dam on the down-side. They keep hold of the stones, of course, by sucking them. Each can carry a stone as large as a hen's egg in this manner. Sometimes Agnatha and Lamprel both take hold of a heavier stone and carry it together.

When the circular nest, three or four feet across, is properly sheltered by the heaped stones, Agnatha and Lamprel go into the place they have prepared. Agnatha lays her eggs and Lamprel pours his milt over them.

What will happen to the young lamper eels that hatch from those eggs? Oh, more interesting things than we have space in this book to tell you about. They will undergo body changes as strange as that of a caterpillar becoming a butterfly or that of a tadpole becoming a frog. They will, in fact, be three or four years old and about five inches long before they can suck a stone like a regular lamprey. Then they will travel down stream from the fresh water of Holiday River to the salt water of Holiday Bay.

You may see them there, perhaps, before they pass on to deeper waters where they will stay until they are as old and as big as Lamprel and Agnatha. And then? Oh, then, of course, they will be ready for nesting time in May.

CHAPTER XII

HARBOR BIRDS

Picnics for Larus, the Gull

LARUS likes to play around with a crowd of other gulls. He does not spend much time alone. There are always a lot of gulls on or near Holiday Shore, and the place suits Larus so well that he stays there most of the year.

If you watch Larus and his comrades performing in the air, you may think that flying is their favorite sport. They can hold out their straight-spread wings and soar higher and higher; and there is no more beautiful sight than gulls sailing against the wind without moving their wings. But however much pleasure the gulls may take in their easy, graceful flight, they never forget to be on the watch for what is an even greater happiness to them—a picnic feast. Breakfast and dinner and supper are all very well, but they are not enough for gulls. They welcome luncheons between meals, too.

So, as they float far overhead, their keen eyes gaze this way and that way. They notice things that move in the water.

Larus, the Gull

During a certain week or two in the spring, for instance, Larus sees thousands of little black sail-shaped objects moving near the surface of the water below him. These objects are really fins on the backs of fishes, called alewives; and the alewives are crowded together in the bay as they turn their tails toward the ocean and head for the fresh water of Holiday Stream.

One glance at the moving fish is enough for Larus. He gives a joyful scream and drops suddenly through the air, alighting on a stone in shallow water. The other gulls repeat his scream and quickly follow him. They speak no words we know, but they sound and act as if they were yelling something that means "Hurrah! Let's go!" Then and there they indulge in a shore dinner of alewife meat.

This ability of gulls to find crowds of fish in the water is sometimes helpful to men. Gulls have a habit of hovering over schools of herring, of swimming among the fish, and of diving to get some to eat. Long ago fishermen named them "Herring Gulls," because by watching these guides they could tell where the herring were running and follow in boats to catch some for themselves.

Although gulls are good enough fishermen to catch small live fish running in schools, their favorite picnics are those where the food is already prepared for them. So they often follow fishing vessels at times when the men are cleaning fish and throwing the waste into the water. They fly close to the boat, screaming loudly as they swoop down for the food. Those that take the smaller pieces can often pick them up while still on the wing, without stopping to settle on the water. But even those that sit down long enough to gobble the larger pieces do not waste much time. In a few minutes they are up in the air again, flying after the fishing vessel, and screaming for more.

Larus and his comrades often follow passenger steamers out of the harbor to see if waste food is thrown overboard. Perhaps next time you take a boat trip you may remember Larus and toss a crust of bread into the water for him as you leave the dock.

Gulls like the same kinds of meat and cooked vegetables that people do, but they are not at all particular that their food should be fresh. They will even take city garbage that is dumped from scows into the water—and like it. Any bird or other animal that eats very stale food is called a scavenger. The scavenger gulls perform a great service in keeping decaying matter out of the way of animals that cannot remain healthy in unclean places. They help keep the seashore and the harbor sanitary, and one of the names given them is "Harbor Gulls."

Some of the picnics are enjoyed several miles from the shore when the gulls go to the meadows to catch grasshoppers. Sometimes these birds go berrying, too, for they like to pick the sweet blueberries that grow on the hillsides not far away.

But what is Larus doing now? There he goes, flying up from the shore with a clam in his beak. He hovers high above the rocks and drops his clam. Then he darts after it with almost the speed of an arrow. He has need to hurry in order to get the meat out of the broken clam shell before another gull can get there to grab it. (You may know that crows have this same famous trick of dropping clams on rocks to break the shells.)

With so much to interest him there you can easily see why Larus plays about Holiday Shore most of the year. There comes a time in the spring, however, when the voice of Larus takes on a different note. He still screams as harshly and eagerly as ever at mealtime when he rushes for food with the crowd. But during more leisurely moments he may be seen strutting up and down the beach while he lifts and lowers his head and gives a long, loud call.

His call has rather an appealing sound. Mrs. Larus, at least, seems to like it. Last spring she listened to it for a week or more; then she and Larus flew away from the shore, to an island far out in Holiday Bay. Hundreds of other gulls followed them, and all soon were working on homes built among the rocky cliffs of the island.

It did not take much time to arrange the nest. A hollow place in a stone served for the floor. A few sticks and a soft padding of grass and other plants made a good bed on which Mrs. Larus laid three eggs. They were grayish blue in color, speckled with lilac and brown.

Both parents helped keep the eggs warm, Larus taking his turn when Mrs. Larus flew away for food. After nearly four weeks of such care the eggs hatched. The downy youngsters were yellow-buff with their underparts nearly white and their backs quite dark and spotted with black.

The little triplets could run about on their pretty dark pink feet almost as soon as they were out of the eggshells; and by the time they were two or three hours old they had already found pleasant shady places among the rocks to hide while they were waiting for their mother or father to bring them something to eat.

Larus did not carry food to his young in his bill as a parent robin does. He swallowed what he found

A downy infant gull among the rocks

and carried it to the island in his stomach. When he reached his family he got the food back into his mouth with a sort of pumping motion of his stomach muscles. Then he laid it on the ground and the youngsters helped themselves. Or perhaps they were in such a hurry that they began to eat by reaching into his mouth with their little bills for some of it there.

Father and Mother Larus were kept very busy for the next five or six weeks, for young gulls are even hungrier than old gulls, which is saying a good deal. By the end of that time, however, the greedy youngsters were large and strong enough to fly and swim for their own food.

There being no longer any reason for staying on the nesting island, Father and Mother Larus and the

107

other old gulls returned to the neighborhood of Holiday Shore.

Yes, those two gulls sitting on the cliff now are Larus and his mate. They look alike, do they not? As you see, their heads and tails and all their under feathers are pure white. Their backs have a bluish-gray color that is sometimes called "gull blue." Their wings are "gull blue" above except for some black and white feathers.

Who is that bird that has the same size and shape as Larus but with quite different colors? Oh, that is one of the Larus youngsters. His suits will be all mottled and streaked with ash-gray, buff, and brown until his third year or later. Then he will dress in feathers like those of his parents.

Whistler and Quandy

Although Larus keeps chiefly to his own Gull Society, he meets many other harbor birds in the course of the year. On chilly winter days, for instance, he may often pass Golden-Eyes, the sea ducks, swimming along the coast.

Father Golden-Eye whistles—not with his mouth but with his wings. As he flies he moves his wings with strong upward and downward strokes. He spreads the long stiff feathers at the tips of his wings as he does so. The air rushes between these stiff feathers with a musical whistling sound as his wings beat rapidly downward. Men who hear such a duck in his flight say, "There goes the Whistler!" That is how Father Golden-Eye got his nickname.

Just how Mother Golden-Eye came by the name of Quandy we cannot tell you; but it takes only a glance at these handsome ducks to know why they are called "Golden-Eyes."

Whistler's spring suit is white underneath. Some of his top feathers are also white. The dark parts of his body, except his head, are gray or sooty brown. His puffy head looks black if he is some distance away; but if he is near enough you can see a beautiful dark, glossy green color with some violet reflections. He has a rather large, rounded, white spot on each side of his head between the eye and the base of his bill. Quandy's head is not quite so puffy, or fluffy, as Whistler's, and it has a plain cinnamon-brown color with no white spot.

Would you like to know where Whistler and Quandy spend their time when they are not wintering off Holiday Shore? Well, last spring, for instance, they flew inland with whistling wings. They went as soon as the water in the streams began to run and the ice was melting in lakes and ponds. Some of the Golden-Eyes who had been their winter companions traveled northward almost far enough to reach Arctic places. Others stopped here and there in Canada. Quandy and Whistler, however, did not get quite to Canada, for they found a tree in one of our northern states which just suited them.

The tree was a large one and in its trunk was a hole exactly right for their nest. A brook ran by the base of the tree, about thirty feet below the nesting hole.

Many birds line their nests with something soft

Whistler and Quandy

before they lay their eggs. Quandy laid her eggs first on the dry chips in the bottom of the hole and then pulled off enough of her breast feathers to cover them with a downy comforter. It took her nearly two weeks to lay her glossy ash-green eggs for she had a dozen of them. (Some Golden-Eyes lay more than that and some lay as few as five or six.)

After sitting on those twelve eggs most of the time day and night for about twenty days, Quandy had the pleasure of welcoming her brood of youngsters as they broke the shells that had held their growing bodies.

Of course Quandy had had brief recesses during her days of brooding while she went for necessary food and drink; but even so twenty days made a long time for her to live in a hole in a tree instead of swimming freely in the water. She had been quite contented to do so, of course, for nothing would have tempted her away from her eggs. But now that the youngsters were hatched—well, that brook looked very inviting to her!

Quandy waited, however, until the downy little Golden-Eyes were two days old. Then she looked them over carefully and left the nest forever. She had had enough of it. She flew down to the water below the hole and clucked. Her babies heard her call and hurried to the doorway of their nest. Then out they tumbled, one after another. They could not fly, but they flapped their tiny wings as they dropped from the high hole in the tree to the brook beside their mother.

Those babies could not fly but they could swim. They did not even need to learn how. So off they paddled down stream with Quandy. Whistler came and stayed with his family much of the time, too.

The Golden-Eye youngsters thrived so well on food, such as little fish and juicy plants they found by diving in freshwater streams and ponds, that early in the fall they had grown to be as large as their parents. They all looked very much like their mother in their first suits. (The sons will not have glossy green feathers and big white spots on their heads until their second winter.)

When cold weather came the ducks did not mind in the least. They were even quite comfortable sitting in the first snow on the bank. But one morning they found something hard and shiny on top of the pond. They could not get their breakfast. Although they did not suffer from the chill winds, all wrapped up in their feather coats, they did object to going without their meals. So they flew to the open sea where they could swim and dive for little fish and other salt-water food during the winter season.

Mr. and Mrs. Bumblebee Peep

Sandpipers

Besides the sea ducks and other swimming birds Larus meets in the harbor, there are many beach birds who visit Holiday Shore twice a year. Larus is somewhere about as they come and go, but he seems to have no particular interest in them.

People find delight in watching them even if Larus does not. See those little sandpipers over there, for instance. They are also known as sand peeps, or bumblebee peeps. When they are resting you might easily pass along the shore without noticing them at a little distance. They are small, about the size of sparrows, and their little streaked brownish-gray backs do not show clearly against the pebbles or the sand. But you can see the whole flock as they race along the wet sand, following the out-going waves to see what sort of shore dinner they washed up for them.

During four or five weeks each spring these little sandpipers may be seen lingering about Holiday Shore. They have come from farther south where they spent the winter; and they are going to Labrador or other northern places to rear their young bumblebee peeps.

Late in the summer they return, the old sandpipers arriving first and their grown sons and daughters following about a fortnight later. During August and September flocks of these little birds are most common on Holiday Shore, though some stay until nearly or quite all winter.

113

When they are not running along the sand on their almost black stiltlike legs, they seem a leisurely lot. They gather in sleepy flocks, tuck their bills under the feathers on their backs, and doze—each, as likely as not, standing on one leg the while. They may have reason enough to be so sleepy, for perhaps they were awake most of the night before. They often travel by night as well as by day.

*   *   *   *   *   *   *

What time are you going to Holiday Shore for your next visit? Of course there is plenty to interest one at any time of the year, but we should not be surprised to hear you say, "I think I'll choose to go while those little sandpipers are visiting there, too."

www.ingramcontent.com/pod-product-compliance
Lightning Source LLC
Chambersburg PA
CBHW031900090426
42741CB00005B/583